Yes We Can!

**General
and Special
Educators
Collaborating
in a
Professional
Learning
Community**

HEATHER FRIZIELLIE
JULIE A. SCHMIDT
JEANNE SPILLER

Solution Tree | Press
a division of
Solution Tree

555 North Morton Street
Bloomington, IN 47404
800.733.6786 (toll free) / 812.336.7700
FAX: 812.336.7790

email: info@solution-tree.com
solution-tree.com

Visit **go.solution-tree.com/PLCbooks** to download the free reproducibles in this book.

Printed in the United States of America

FSC
www.fsc.org
MIX
Paper from
responsible sources
FSC® C011935

Library of Congress Cataloging-in-Publication Data

Names: Friziellie, Heather, author. | Schmidt, Julie A. author. | Spiller,
    Jeanne, author.
Title: Yes we can! : general and special educators collaborating in a
    professional learning community / Heather Friziellie, Julie A. Schmidt,
    and Jeanne Spiller.
Description: Bloomington, IN : Solution Tree Press, [2016] | Includes
    bibliographical references and index.
Identifiers: LCCN 2015048973 | ISBN 9781936763993 (perfect bound)
Subjects: LCSH: Group work in education. | Professional learning communities.
    | Teachers--In-service training. | Special education
    teachers--Professional relationships.
Classification: LCC LB1032 .F79 2016 | DDC 371.39/5--dc23 LC record available at
    http://lccn.loc.gov/2015048973

Solution Tree
Jeffrey C. Jones, CEO
Edmund M. Ackerman, President

Solution Tree Press
President: Douglas M. Rife
Senior Acquisitions Editor: Amy Rubenstein
Editorial Director: Tonya Cupp
Managing Production Editor: Caroline Weiss
Senior Editor: Kari Gillesse
Copy Editor: Ashante K. Thomas
Proofreader: Jessi Finn
Text and Cover Designer: Rian Anderson

Acknowledgments

I have the distinct privilege of working with extraordinary educators, administrators, board members, parents, and, most importantly, students in Kildeer Countryside Community Consolidated School District 96. Each day, I am awed and inspired by my colleagues' work ethic, knowledge base, innovation, commitment to PLC practices, and passion for making sure *all* learners in our system find success. I learn from them daily and feel lucky to be part of such an amazing school district. On a personal note, I thank my husband, Shaun, and my children, Katie, Braden, and Taylor, for being my constant inspiration and my light in life. You each make me a better person, and I love you more than you'll ever know. Last, to my parents, I thank you for always believing in me and making sure that I grew up to view challenges as opportunities.

—Heather

Becoming a school district superintendent was not something I ever aspired to . . . until I joined the Kildeer District 96 family. I, as most do, feel very passionate about and dedicated to the amazing, ongoing PLC work that we have worked so hard to deeply embed. It is this work and the incredibly talented people at all levels of the organization that changed my mind and my heart. The teachers, support staff, administrators, and board of education members I am privileged to know and serve remind me every day that *all* students can succeed at high levels when the adults in their environment believe they can and provide the supports necessary for them to excel. I am thankful to have parents who believe deeply in public education and who still tell me that they are proud of me every opportunity they get! But no one knows the depth of my commitment to this work better than my husband, Rob, and my daughter, Lily, both of whom I love with all my heart. Their willingness to share me, combined with their unwavering love, support, and patience, make me a better educator, wife, mom, and person.

—Julie

The best years of my teaching career were the three years I co-taught with Amy Lilly, a dedicated and passionate special education teacher. Together, Amy and I set out to ensure that every student in our classroom learned at high levels. We had high expectations for all our students and every single one of them met those expectations. Sure, we worked hard and it wasn't always easy, but watching our students learn, grow, and truly thrive solidified for me that the hours of planning to provide just the right amount of support and scaffolding were worth it. Thank you, Amy, for the experience that shaped me as an educator and started the journey that led to this book.

I consider myself extremely fortunate to work in a school district where we all work hard every day to live up to the ideals in this book. Thank you to Tom Many and Chris Jakicic for believing in me and giving me the opportunity to follow my passion for teaching and learning in a place like Kildeer District 96. I would also like to thank my coauthors, Heather and Julie, for their thoughtful insights, feedback, and support throughout the writing process.

Most importantly, thank you to my husband, Dave, my son, Brandon, and my daughter, Breton, for encouraging me and loving me no matter what.

—Jeanne

Solution Tree Press would like to thank the following reviewers:

Colleen Armstrong
Codirector of Special Education
Webster Central School District
Webster, New York

Crystal Bratton
Special Education Teacher
Bloomington High School North
Bloomington, Indiana

Troy Gago
Middle School Special Education
Teacher
Stanley-Boyd School District
Stanley, Wisconsin

SuAnn Grant
Deputy Superintendent
Fort Leavenworth USD 207
Fort Leavenworth, Kansas

Staci Green
Director of Special Education
Harrison County Co-Op
Hallsville, Texas

Liann Hanson
Principal
Oak Crest Elementary School
Belle Plaine, Minnesota

Kathleen Hugo
Director of Special Education
Monroe County Community School
Corporation
Bloomington, Indiana

Table of Contents

Reproducible pages are in italics.

About the Authors ix

INTRODUCTION   **Improving Outcomes for *All* Students** . .1

How This Book Is Structured 2

Getting the Most Out of This Book 3

PART I   **Closing the Gap Through Collaboration**   **5**

CHAPTER 1   **Understanding the History and Reality of Special Education** .7

Who Are Students With Special Needs? 8

The President's Commission on Excellence in Special Education 9

Essential Beliefs About Student Learning and Collective Responsibility 14

Commitment to Closing the Gap .16

Yes We Can: Keys to Moving Forward 16

CHAPTER 2   **Collaborating for *All* Students** 17

Working Together in Elementary Teams 17

Working Together in Secondary Teams 24

Fusing Collaboration and Professional Development 27

Yes We Can: Keys to Moving Forward 28

CHAPTER 3   **Developing a Culture of Shared Learning Expectations** 29

Establishing a School Culture That Supports All Students 33

Ensuring That All Students Learn at High Levels 36

Yes We Can: Keys to Moving Forward 37

PART II   Closing the Gap Through a Focus on Learning and Results   39

CHAPTER 4   **Establishing What All Students Should Learn** 41

Eliminating Curriculum Chaos and Taking Action. 42

Selecting an Upcoming Unit or Topic and Deciding What Students
Should Know and Be Able to Do 44

Prioritizing the List of What Students Should Know and Be Able to Do 45

Unpacking the Priority Standards. 46

Yes We Can: Keys to Moving Forward 62

CHAPTER 5   **Designing Standards-Aligned Instruction for Student Success** .63

Defining Instructional Shifts 63

Tailoring Instruction for Students With Special Needs 66

Yes We Can: Keys to Moving Forward 72

CHAPTER 6   **Determining Criteria for Assessment**. 75

Aligning Instruction and Assessment. 78

Developing the Assessment 79

Designing a Specialized Curriculum 80

Yes We Can: Keys to Moving Forward 81

CHAPTER 7   **Planning Goals and Monitoring Progress for All Learners** 83

Planning Goals and Monitoring Growth 85

Fine-Tuning Progress Monitoring for Struggling Learners 92

Collecting Data Aligned to Goals. 95

Yes We Can: Keys to Moving Forward 95

CHAPTER 8   **Responding When Students Don't Learn** 97

Examining Response to Intervention Legislation 98

Making Connections Between RTI and PLCs. 100

Improving Core Instruction to Close the Gap 100

Connecting RTI and PLC Practices for Special Education Students 102

Yes We Can: Keys to Moving Forward 106
Final Thoughts 106

Appendix A: Reproducibles 109

Simple as 1, 2, 3: The Prioritizing Process *110*
Unpacking Document *112*
Protocol to Focus Standards-Based IEP Goals *113*
Content Area of Focus *114*
Individual Problem-Solving Discussion Guide *115*

Appendix B: Glossary 117

References and Resources 121

Index 127

Vist **go.solution-tree.com/PLCbooks** to
download the free reproducibles in this book.

About the Authors

Heather Friziellie is director of educational services for Kildeer Countryside Community Consolidated School District 96, located in Buffalo Grove, Illinois. She previously served as both an elementary and middle school principal. As a leader, she is involved in literacy curriculum development, data analysis, and staff development. With experience as a building- and district-level administrator, curriculum specialist, and classroom teacher, Heather has consulted with districts throughout the United States and presented at national conferences. Educators at all levels have benefited from her insight and experience related to developing high-performing teams, data-driven decision making, response to intervention (RTI), and literacy instruction. She received a Those Who Excel award in Illinois in the School Administrator category.

Heather earned a master's degree in curriculum and instruction with an endorsement in school administration and a bachelor's degree in elementary education. She is pursuing a doctorate.

To learn more about Heather's work, visit www.kcsd96.org and http://edservices scoop.blogspot.com, and follow her on Twitter @heatherlfriz.

Julie A. Schmidt is superintendent of schools for Kildeer Countryside Community Consolidated School District 96 in Buffalo Grove, Illinois. The district began its professional learning community (PLC) journey in 2000, remains focused on the work, and is recognized on AllThingsPLC. Schools in District 96 have received five U.S. Department of Education Blue Ribbon Awards of Excellence—three during her tenure as superintendent. During more than twenty-six years in education, Julie has been a superintendent, an associate superintendent, a high school director of student services, a school psychologist, an assistant to the superintendent, and an assistant director of special education spanning early childhood through high school. She continues to work with elementary and secondary schools across the United States. A respected speaker and facilitator,

Julie focuses on RTI, leadership and change, and the implementation of PLC practices at all levels of an organization. Julie serves on the national PLC advisory board for Solution Tree.

Julie received the Principals' Award of Excellence during her service at the high school level, where she also earned the Administrative Award of Excellence. As a member of the Illinois Association of School Administrators, Julie serves on three state-level committees: Illinois Balanced Accountability, Professional Development, and Vision 20/20. She was nominated for and elected to membership in Suburban School Superintendents, which offers membership to no more than 150 superintendents across the United States. She also serves as the Lake County Superintendents professional development chair and as president of the executive board of the Exceptional Learners Collaborative, of which District 96 is a founding member.

Julie earned a bachelor's degree from St. Mary's University in San Antonio, Texas, and a master's degree and a specialist degree from Southwest Texas State University in San Marcos, Texas (now Texas State University). She has completed doctoral coursework at both Roosevelt University and Northern Illinois University.

To learn more about Julie's work, follow her on Twitter @kildeer96.

Jeanne Spiller is assistant superintendent for teaching and learning for Kildeer Countryside Community Consolidated School District 96 in Buffalo Grove, Illinois. Her work focuses on implementation of standards-aligned instruction and assessment practices. She guides the process of unpacking, powering, scaling, and pacing standards for numerous schools, districts, and teacher teams. She is passionate about collaborating with schools to develop systems for teaching and learning that keep the focus on student results and help teachers determine how to approach instruction so that all students learn at high levels.

Jeanne has served as a classroom teacher, building staff developer, team leader, and middle school assistant principal. She is the former president of the Illinois affiliate of Learning Forward and serves on its board of directors.

Jeanne earned a master's degree in educational teaching and leadership from Saint Xavier University, a master's degree in educational administration from Loyola University Chicago, and an educational administrative superintendent endorsement from Northern Illinois University.

To learn more about Jeanne's work, follow her on Twitter @jeeneemarie.

To book Heather Friziellie, Julie A. Schmidt, or Jeanne Spiller for professional development, contact pd@solution-tree.com.

INTRODUCTION

Improving Outcomes for *All* Students

If a child cannot learn in the way we teach, we must teach in a way the child can learn.

—Unknown

In working with schools and districts across the United States on improving outcomes for all students through the implementation of professional learning community (PLC) practices, we have been struck by the lack of clear definitions and expectations for the role and place of special education in the PLC process.

Given the clear and pervasive gap in achievement between general education and special education students, the purpose of *Yes We Can!* is to examine the collaborative partnership between general and special education in maximizing learning for all students. As the United States and all school systems move to adopt more rigorous standards, this book will focus on applying PLC practices to fully include special education and special educators in the planning and delivery of standards-aligned curriculum, instruction, and assessment. These aims will be explored through the lens of the key PLC tenets, with specific strategies and methods outlined so that the reader can put to use the contents as well as demonstrate an increased understanding of how special education fits within a PLC.

PLC experts Richard DuFour, Rebecca DuFour, Robert Eaker, and Thomas W. Many (2010) define a PLC as:

> an ongoing process in which educators work collaboratively in recurring cycles of collective inquiry and action research to achieve better results for the students they serve. Professional learning communities operate under the assumption that the key to improved learning for students is continuous job-embedded learning for educators. (p. 11)

Further, they note that the work of PLCs is guided by three big ideas (a focus on learning, a collaborative culture, and a results orientation) and four critical questions.

1. What is it we expect our students to learn?

2. How will we know when they have learned it?

3. How will we respond when some students do not learn?

4. How will we respond when some students already know it?

Going forward, we will refer to these tenets of PLCs as the *three big ideas* and the *four critical questions*.

We believe there are not clear expectations for including special education in the work of a PLC and, more important, about what needs to be done in order to impact learning outcomes for our most at-risk students. Too often, we find that special education is neither part of collaborative processes nor addressed in the work of answering the four critical questions. We also recognize that including special education in all parts of the PLC process requires significant shifts in belief systems as well as structures. We address these shifts in thinking as well as outline key action steps for changing structures to match the mindset that *all* students can learn.

How This Book Is Structured

Yes We Can! is presented in two parts: (1) "Closing the Gap Through Collaboration" and (2) "Closing the Gap Through a Focus on Learning and Results". Each part presents vital information that teams within a PLC need to know to foster an environment of learning for *all* students. In both parts, all chapters conclude with keys to moving forward in the collective endeavor to close the gap for students with special needs.

Part I, which includes chapters 1–3, focuses on the history behind the divide between general and special education, and the ways PLCs can shift mindsets to establish a culture of shared responsibility for all students' learning. Chapter 1 surveys the history of special education in the United States to help readers understand the legislation, policies, and changes that have influenced special education. Chapter 2 proposes an alternative to the divide between general and special education by illustrating how powerful collaboration between general and special educators can close the gap for even the neediest students, those who are the most discrepant learners because they are at risk or significantly impaired. It explains several forms teams at the elementary and secondary levels may take to ensure that general and special educators work together to improve learning outcomes for all students. Chapter 3 guides educators to commit to a shared responsibility to ensure that all students learn and outlines three action steps that teachers can take to ensure a guaranteed and viable curriculum for all students.

Part II, covering chapters 4–8, shows collaborative teams within PLCs how to close the achievement gap by focusing on learning and on results. Grounded in the three big ideas and four critical questions of a PLC, part II teaches general and special educators how to tailor instruction, plan assessments, create goals, and monitor progress to ensure that all students receive the support they need to learn. Chapter 4 examines the roles of general and special educators in determining what they want students to know and be able to do. To help educators come to a common agreement in answering this critical question, this chapter provides a tool to assist teams in unpacking standards to guide expectations for learning outcomes. Chapter 5 builds on the learning targets identified in the unpacking process by offering strategies for designing standards-aligned instruction for all learners and for tailoring instruction when needed for students with special needs. Chapter 6 demonstrates how collaborative teams can align standards-based instruction and assessment for all learners. In chapter 7, protocols assist collaborative teams in using assessment data to plan and refine goals and to monitor progress. Chapter 8 outlines response to intervention (RTI) structures and practices to show teams how to respond when students don't learn.

Yes We Can! concludes with two appendices. Appendix A features reproducible versions of the many tools and templates mentioned throughout the chapters. Appendix B is a glossary of terms commonly used when discussing PLCs, RTI, students with special needs, and related topics. If we know anything, we know that the use of terms and acronyms is particularly prevalent in the world of special education. So, too, is it widespread in the world of teaching and learning. Please note that throughout this text, we choose to use the term *students with special needs.*

Getting the Most Out of This Book

Yes We Can! is intended for general education teachers, special education teachers, related-services providers, principals, and central office administrators. Whether the reader is working to embed PLC tenets to positively impact student learning or is strictly focused on closing the achievement gap, the content will be meaningful and relevant. Through this framework, neither special educators nor administrators will be able to contend that the work does not apply to them or even that special education is helpless to embed PLC practices in systems that do not currently work as PLCs. To be clear, the strategies we discuss throughout this text apply to *all* learners; however, our focus in this book is to examine practices that support students with special needs. Only after we begin to make strides toward shifting mindsets, reconsidering structures, and truly collaborating at high levels focused on the learning of all students will we begin to see steady and sustainable progress toward closing the gaps.

PART I

CLOSING THE GAP THROUGH COLLABORATION

CHAPTER 1

UNDERSTANDING THE HISTORY AND REALITY OF SPECIAL EDUCATION

> *Although it is true that special education has created a base of civil rights and legal protections, children with special needs remain those most at risk of being left behind. The facts create a sense of urgency for reform that few can deny.*
>
> —President's Commission on Excellence in Special Education

The sense of urgency in the President's Commission on Excellence in Special Education (2002) report has not dissipated for our most at-risk students. In fact, progress toward closing this gap made under old standards and less rigorous accountability assessments has all but vanished. Schools and school districts across the United States are feverishly working toward the implementation of new, more rigorous learning standards for *all* students. This new, higher level of accountability has challenged schools that have stalled in improvement efforts as well as those that have been deemed high-performing. As the bar is raised, closing the gap feels further and further out of reach for our most disadvantaged students. But without sufficient support for the implementation of more rigorous learning standards, schools are in danger of letting students, especially those with special needs, fall through the cracks, setting them up for a cycle of low expectations, struggle, and failure. As educators, we know that for students who have historically struggled in school, an adult life full of financial and societal challenges likely awaits, so it is crucial schools ensure that learning for all includes students served through special education.

Historically, students with special needs "drop out of high school at twice the rate of their peers," and the enrollment rate for special needs students in higher education "is nearly 50 percent lower than enrollment among the general population" (President's Commission, 2002, p. 3). While some progress has been made with the "overall percentage of students with a learning disability who drop out declining from 35 percent in 2002 to 19 percent in 2011" (Cortiella & Horowitz, 2014), the dropout rate for all students has declined from 10.5 percent to 7.1 percent during that same time frame (Stark, Noel, & McFarland, 2015). But little attention has been paid over the years by federal accountability systems to whether those students are advancing in core subjects or acquiring the skills necessary for making special education and accommodations no longer necessary (Lyon et al., 2001). Special education administrators report that despite the overly burdensome compliance issues attached to special education, they have never been asked to report how many students no longer qualify for services in a given year. In fact, a very small percentage of those who qualify for special education actually ever move out of the services. Some researchers indicate that "students who enter special education with reading levels that are two or more years below those of their age mates can be expected to maintain that disparity, or fall further behind" (Denton, Vaughn, & Fletcher, 2003, p. 203). So while schools across the United States have struggled to provide students with the most intensive help available, the achievement gap has continued to grow. Over a thirty-year span, achievement gaps in reading and mathematics between general and special education students, as measured by accountability assessments nationally, have reached 40 percent and 50 percent, even in some high-performing areas (National Center for Education Statistics, n.d.). Sadly, minority students have been disproportionately identified in some categories of special education, and the number of all special education students identified as having a specific learning disability has grown more than 300 percent from the passage of the Individuals With Disabilities Education Act (IDEA) through 2006 with some pattern of trending downward since the passage of response to intervention legislation (Cortiella & Horowitz, 2014; President's Commission, 2002).

Who Are Students With Special Needs?

Before we address the need to ensure high levels of learning for all students, let's examine who our students with special needs are. Table 1.1 illustrates the distribution of students served under each eligibility category the U.S. Department of Education's (n.d.) Office of Special Education database reports through 2011.

Table 1.1 illustrates that most of these students by definition do not have a significant cognitive disability (McNulty & Gloeckler, 2011). To be more specific, 80 to 85 percent of identified students have no cognitive impairment (Cortiella & Horowitz, 2014). Unfortunately, the results of a 2012 survey conducted by the National Center for Learning Disabilities (Cortiella & Horowitz, 2014) indicate that 43 percent of the general public wrongly believe that learning disabilities are correlated with IQ or intelligence. The survey's results lead us to wonder about past and current mindsets about the learning potential of students identified as having a learning disability. Misconceptions about students with disabilities make our mission two-pronged: we must shift our practices to ensure high levels of learning and make significant cultural shifts.

Table 1.1: Distribution of Students With Special Needs in the United States

Disability	Percentage
Learning disabilities	42 percent
Speech or language impairments	19 percent
Other health impairments	13 percent
Intellectual disabilities	8 percent
Autism	7 percent
Emotional disturbance	6 percent
All others	5 percent

Sources: McNulty & Gloeckler, 2011; U.S. Department of Education, n.d.

The President's Commission on Excellence in Special Education

Although we have a long way to go, steps toward shifting educators' practices to ensure high levels of learning and establishing the culture to support that aim began many years ago. On October 2, 2001, President George W. Bush created the President's Commission on Excellence in Special Education, and in July 2002, the commission released its findings and recommendations in its report, *A New Area: Revitalizing Special Education for Children and Their Families*. The historical context of special education is important to understanding the reasons behind our recommendations, and it is from the commission's report that some of the most compelling catalysts for change have originated.

The commission's findings include that, often, qualifying for special education becomes an endpoint and not a gateway to more effective instruction and targeted, specific intervention. The report reiterates that cases of students qualifying for special education services, moving into the special education system, and receiving the intensive services needed to close the gap and no longer necessitate specialized instruction and supports, are few and far between (President's Commission, 2002).

The report also indicates that the system is "wait to fail" instead of a model based on prevention and intervention. This finding speaks to the long-known flaws in identifying learning disabilities and the use of the antiquated discrepancy model. For years, educators have seen students entering first grade who struggled with preliteracy and literacy development. By mid–first grade, the discrepancy became pronounced between what these struggling students learned and what standards other students were mastering. In our collective experience as authors, facilitators, and practitioners, we would see these students historically referred to the traditional prereferral intervention team that would decide who would be evaluated for special education eligibility and when they would be evaluated. If the evidence was compelling, the educational team *may* have proceeded with a full case study evaluation. However, in a discrepancy model, the likelihood of detecting a statistically significant difference between first graders' IQ scores and their scores on any given subtest on an achievement battery are slim. For years, teams have heard the results of such evaluations include statements like, "If he is still not making adequate progress by the middle of second grade, we'll reconsider his case." Essentially, the results indicated that the gap between him and his peers was not yet statistically significant enough in order to qualify for more help. Therefore, the team would have to wait another school year so that the gap got wider and we could make the student eligible for the services that he or she needed. This not only sounds illogical, but the strategy stands in stark contrast to research surrounding the importance of early intervention, as synthesized by Karen E. Diamond, Laura M. Justice, Robert S. Siegler, and Patricia A. Snyder (2013). However, if there was nothing available in a school or a system other than the strategies individual teachers used in isolation or the special education system, our choice was special education. In the past, it was the best and only option to provide access to more time for learning and more intensive instruction. All teachers who see students failing to develop the skills they need want the most intensive help available to those students in the system.

Unfortunately, by the time the discrepancy model detects the statistically significant difference necessary for eligibility, students are much more than one year behind. In fact, the commission's findings indicate that many identification methods lack validity and thousands of students are misidentified each year. This speaks not only to the flaws in the discrepancy model but to the widely varying and often subjective eligibility criteria applied across the United States. With the 2004 reauthorization of IDEA, states are no longer required to use the discrepancy model to identify students who qualify for special education services. Reactions to this update vary, ranging from no change in practice to states banning the use of the discrepancy model.

Another concern the commission reports is that educators and policymakers alike think about special education and general education as two systems, when in fact, general and special education share responsibilities and should not be considered separate. Thinking of general and special education as two systems contributes to the "those are your students and these are my students" mentality. Thus, the reality was—and continues to be in many schools—that a special system of education and a general system of education exist separately, and never shall the two meet. A shared accountability for the learning of *all* students was, and continues to be, woefully absent. A litany of issues contribute to the division of general and special education and to the lack of shared accountability for all students.

- A required and burdensome focus on special educators' compliance with procedural safeguards that detract from a laserlike focus on student learning

- The absence of collaborative structures and schedules that allow regular collaboration and communication between general and special educators

- The tendency for students in a special education instructional setting to work on a parallel curriculum that does not focus on grade-level standards

- Traditional "push out" models that require that special education–eligible students leave the mainstream classroom in order to receive core content instruction

The commission also finds that students with special needs require highly qualified teachers. Since the release of the commission's report, the term *highly qualified* has become commonly used. Unfortunately, both general and special education teacher preparation programs have historically paid too little attention to research and best practices in literacy and mathematics instruction. The gaps do not stop once newly prepared teachers graduate. Special education teachers were and are hired to help all students learn at high levels, yet the schools and districts that hire them often do not support their continuing education. While general education teachers participate in professional development on best practices in literacy and mathematics instruction, special education teachers, who quite often teach core content, are relegated to the special education office, spending their professional development time making sure they are in compliance with procedural safeguards. When we, as authors and facilitators, talk about this particular finding in rooms full of special education teachers and related-services personnel, they nod in acknowledgment of the fact that they are rarely included in those rich, job-embedded conversations about understanding learning targets and best instructional practices to teach to those targets. How this has ever made sense is baffling.

The commission also reports that the system does not always embrace or implement evidence-based practices. If a knowing-doing gap exists in the general education realm, and we contend it does, it also exists in the special education realm. These findings led the commission to make three major recommendations.

1. **Focus more on results and focus less on process:** Because special educators must spend so much time dealing with processes and procedures, they are left with very little time to examine student data in such a way that instruction and student goals can be altered. The overabundance of processes and procedures is a barrier to focusing on student growth and to participating in meaningful professional development on instructional practices.

2. **Embrace a model of prevention and not a model of failure:** Since the report's release, there has been a tidal wave of support for early intervening, both in the reauthorization of IDEA in 2004 and the passage of RTI legislation thereafter. With that legislation comes a move away from the use of the antiquated discrepancy model. Yet, since the publication of the President's Commission (2002) report, there has only been a 3 percent decline in the number of students becoming eligible for and entering into the special education system across the United States (Cortiella & Horowitz, 2014).

3. **Think of students with special needs as general education students first and special education students second in classrooms and in boardrooms:** Only when this belief becomes deeply embedded into the culture of our schools and districts will we begin to see evidence of collective responsibility for the learning of *all* students.

So if the longitudinal data and new expectations create a new sense of urgency, it begs the question, What are effective schools doing to achieve dramatic results in student learning? Robert J. Marzano (2003) finds that "an analysis of research conducted over a thirty-five-year period demonstrates that the schools that are highly effective produce results that almost entirely overcome the effects of student backgrounds" (p. 7). We assert that deep implementation of PLC practices is the pathway to highly effective schools that improve outcomes for *all* students.

For example, in Kildeer Countryside Community Consolidated School District 96 in Buffalo Grove, Illinois, the gap between special education and general education students had been closing at a steady pace between 2005 and 2013. In fact, under the old Illinois Learning Standards, which had not been updated since 1997, the percentage of special education–eligible students who were meeting standards grew 21.8 percent over seven years in the area of reading and 20.4 percent in mathematics on the Illinois Standards Achievement Test (ISAT). Figures 1.1 and 1.2 illustrate the steady progress from 2003 to 2012. Overall student outcomes improved every year for thirteen straight years for all students, and the gap between general and special education populations began to shrink significantly as the district implemented and more deeply embedded the PLC framework and the shifts in mindset outlined in this book from 2005 to 2013.

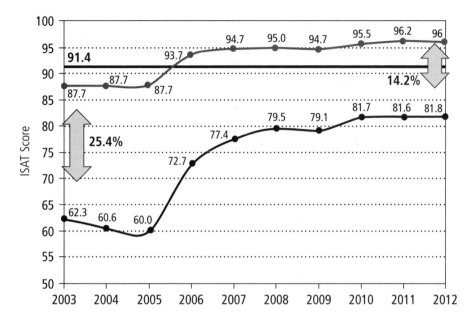

Source: Kildeer Countryside Community Consolidated School District 96, Buffalo Grove, Illinois.

Note: The gray line represents the accountability results in reading for all students. The black line represents the accountability results in reading for special education eligible students only.

Figure 1.1: Reading progress, 2003–2012.

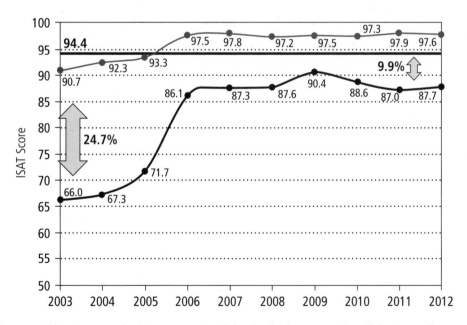

Source: Kildeer Countryside Community Consolidated School District 96, Buffalo Grove, Illinois.

Note: The gray line represents the accountability results in mathematics for all students. The black line represents the accountability results in mathematics for special education eligible students only.

Figure 1.2: Mathematics progress, 2003–2012.

With the adoption of the National Governors Association Center for Best Practices (NGA) and the Council of Chief State School Officers' (CCSSO) Common Core State Standards (CCSS) initiative and more rigorous standards across the United States, the bar for meeting standards has been elevated, thus creating a renewed sense of urgency for all. If systems were making progress toward closing the gap, their goal-setting processes must be revamped with vigor. If the significant gap was constant, it has only gotten worse. But the good news is, as illustrated by this district, it is possible to close the gap.

While we rarely encounter a school or a district that began the PLC journey solely in order to close the gap between special education and general education students, deep implementation that results in teams continuously working to answer the four critical questions improves outcomes for all. In fact, Jon Saphier (2005) contends:

> The reason professional learning communities increase student learning is that they produce more good teaching by more teachers more of the time. Put simply, PLCs improve teaching, which improves student results, especially for the least advantaged of students. (p. 23)

The cultural shift needed to implement the PLC framework successfully requires that systems, schools, and teams examine two critical beliefs about learning: (1) all students can learn at high levels, and (2) teams must take collective responsibility for the learning of *all* students. These core beliefs must remain at the forefront of decision-making processes to improve learning outcomes for all students. Because they are critical factors to guide learning, it is worthwhile to examine where your system, school, or team stands in adopting these tenets. Next, let's explore how these essential beliefs influence learning outcomes for all students.

Essential Beliefs About Student Learning and Collective Responsibility

First, consider that all students can learn at high levels. As districts, schools, and teams begin to openly discuss mindset and beliefs about student learning, the first word that often emerges after affirming that all students can learn is *but*: "Of course I believe all students can learn, *but . . . .*" And invariably, someone in the room will raise his or her hand to ask, "Can you define what you mean by *all*?" Interesting question. It always causes us to pause no matter how many times it is asked. *All* really does mean *all*. We will dig deeper into this in chapter 3.

We contend that educators' expectations and mindsets impact what students will master. The battle ahead is clearly indicated in the commission's survey results regarding perception of students' learning abilities. Martha L. Thurlow (2011), the director of the National Center on Educational Outcomes, reminds educators the reality is that:

> Some students—with and without special needs—may not achieve the levels we hope even after high quality standards-based instruction. But we have no way to predict which ones will not achieve high levels of learning; thus, we have to teach them ALL well.

Thurlow and colleagues Rachel F. Quenemoen and Sheryl S. Lazarus (2012) go on to say that "the preponderance of evidence is that the *system* is responsible for limited access to the general curriculum and the resulting achievement gap—not the student's disabilities, color, socioeconomic status, or other characteristics" (p. 11). Whatever excuse is given, educators have a responsibility to meet all learners' needs. Given the complexity of this task, we will discuss a plan for decision making in chapter 3 that addresses even the most severely disabled students.

Second, remember that teams must share collective responsibility for all students' learning. This belief can readily be observed and assessed in systems. No matter who the classroom teacher is or who is responsible for core instruction, all teachers in the school take ownership of every student mastering targets. For example, on a third-grade team, the entire team is responsible for all third-grade students' learning. How well the team works collaboratively and assumes collective responsibility for all students' learning often come to light when students with special needs struggle. It is all too common that everyone looks to the special education teacher or case manager to fix the problem. This tendency is so deeply embedded in some systems that when a special education student struggles with multiple content areas or behavioral skills, it becomes the special education teacher's and related-services personnel's responsibility to address. In one session during a PLC institute, a participant shared that her school had made strides related to collective responsibility. As a special education teacher, she was invited to grade-level team meetings. She was, however, required to remove all her special education students' data when the team set and monitored SMART goals. So while the school made strides in ensuring that general and special education teachers were both involved in collaborative team meetings and even in conversations about instructional practices, the commitment came to a halt. Including special education–student data in goal setting was a level of collective responsibility that had not yet been embraced. Thus, the message to special education teachers is that while *they* can be part of the conversation, their students' outcomes cannot. In a culture where collective responsibility is deeply embedded, discussions about goals and outcomes include every student in every seat in the classroom.

Commitment to Closing the Gap

Creating a sense of urgency to do the right work in the right way means creating high standards of beliefs about something that is vitally important—a moral imperative. As educators fully commit to a cycle of continuous improvement in schools and grapple with decisions related to priorities, they must hold themselves accountable to a critically important question: What do they want for every student in their school? When they think about a student who is precious to them, whether that is a son, daughter, niece, nephew, or grandchild, is the improvement they are considering something they would want for that special child? Because if it is, then it is something that they should want for every student in every seat in every classroom in their school or system. We have seen building-level leaders drive this point home by asking every faculty member at the beginning of a school year to bring in a picture of a child who is precious to him or her. They display those pictures on a board in the faculty lounge with the heading "Is It Good Enough for Them?" Each day when adults enter the lounge, they are faced with that question, keeping it in the forefront of their minds when they are deep in the work.

Elementary and secondary schools both need to consider the extent to which they make decisions and take action in accordance with the beliefs that all students can learn at high levels and that everyone in the school has a collective responsibility for all students' learning. These beliefs may be acting as the proverbial elephant in the room. By identifying the barriers to successful learning outcomes for all students, educators can begin to make the cultural shifts that will lead to closing the gaps among all subgroups of students.

Yes We Can: Keys to Moving Forward

Many changes have influenced special education legislation and policies. As you think about special education policies and practices in your own school or district, keep in mind the following keys to moving forward.

- Acknowledge and share the evolution of special education in order to frame the *why* behind future work.

- Examine special education incidence rates locally to understand the distribution and trends over time.

- Conduct a gap analysis using both local and accountability assessment data to determine your areas of greatest need.

- Share the gap analysis data with *all* educators in order to frame a collective responsibility mindset.

In chapter 2, we turn our attention to the ways general and special educators can work together to close the gap for students with special needs.

CHAPTER 2

COLLABORATING FOR *ALL* STUDENTS

*Teacher collaboration in strong professional learning commu-
nities improves the quality and equity of student learning, pro-
motes discussions that are grounded in evidence and analysis
rather than opinion, and fosters collective responsibility for
student success.*

—Milbrey W. McLaughlin and Joan E. Talbert

High-performing collaborative teams' impact on student learning is well documented in research (see, for example, Barth, 1991; Little, 1990, 2006;
McLaughlin & Talbert, 2006). But digging deeper into those teams' structure
and membership sheds light not only on the question, Does *all* really mean *all*? but
also on exactly how serious we are about closing the gap for our students. Structures
that include special education personnel can only go so far without mutual accountability for meaningful agenda items and conversation.

Working Together in Elementary Teams

In schools and districts where the practice of excluding special educators from
learning teams is well entrenched, it may be difficult to imagine new structures that
allow for genuine collaboration. Table 2.1 (page 18) illustrates some common team
structures at the elementary level.

As educators reconsider how schedules and teams are structured to best support all students, one of the changes they may need to address is how caseloads
are assigned. In one elementary school, one special education teacher would take
responsibility for resource and self-contained core content instruction in literacy
for grades 1–5, and another special education teacher would take responsibility for
resource and self-contained core content instruction in mathematics for grades 1–5.

Table 2.1: Potential Elementary Teams

	Grade-Level Teams	Leadership Teams (Building-Level Teams)	Problem-Solving and Intervention Teams (Building-Level Teams)	Job-Alike, Cross-School Teams
Who	*All* teachers within the same grade level within the school	Team leader from each grade-level team to include specials, intervention team, and so on	Principal, related-services personnel, English learner or representative, teacher representative, special education teachers	A teacher representative from each grade-level team to each content area
Focus	• Students (celebration and problem solving) • Planning • Common assessments • Data analysis • Instructional design and planning • Intervention design	• Building-level problem solving • Implementation of district and school initiatives and goals • Team-level communication	• RTI implementation • Problem-solving process • Progress monitoring	• Power standards • Pacing guides • Benchmark assessments • Materials selection • Instructional design and planning • Data analysis
Frequency	Twice per week during common planning time	Once per week	Once per week	Monthly

As mindsets began to shift in the school's culture and a collective responsibility for the learning of all students became deeply embedded, grade-level teams wondered how to be truly committed to high levels of learning for all students when teachers responsible for core content instruction and reinforcement were not at the table. Thus, in this particular school, teams restructured areas of responsibility so that one special education teacher took responsibility for resource and core content instruction for both literacy and mathematics in grades 1–2, and the other teacher took responsibility for resource and core content instruction in literacy and mathematics in grades 3–5. This increased each special education teacher's ability to sit on and be a real member of those grade-level teams on an ongoing basis.

In this culture of mutual accountability, grade-level teams purposefully structured their agendas in a way that ensured that the special education teacher would be involved in the most critical student learning conversations. When the special education teacher could not be at a grade-level team meeting, a general education teacher took responsibility for communication through informal and formal conversations, as well as electronic communications via Google Docs (www.google.com/docs). Of course, the elementary school's approach is just one example of how schools can structure teams to include special educators. Let's examine the structure and roles of each type of team outlined in table 2.1 more closely.

Reconsidering Grade-Level Teams

When examining elementary collaborative teams' structure and membership, the first team we turn to is the grade-level team, where deep, job-embedded conversations happen about instructional strategies, data analysis, and intervention. For example, is the educator responsible for third-grade special education students regularly attending third-grade collaborative team meetings, and is he or she a true member of the team? If we are truly committed to keeping special education–entitled students at appropriate grade-level standards, it is critical that all teachers responsible for those students' learning are involved in the conversation.

The team structure illustrated in table 2.1 often requires that an elementary school move to a master schedule. (Consult Buffum & Mattos, 2015; Mattos & Buffum, 2015, for more on effective master schedules.) An elementary master schedule means that all first-grade teachers teach literacy at the same time and all first-grade teachers teach mathematics at the same time. While master schedules can be a controversial topic at the elementary level, they offer a way to maximize our use of time and resources. In this structured schedule, all first graders go to lunch, recess, specials, and so on at the same time, thus creating more opportunity for first-grade teacher collaboration. In addition, this schedule allows related-services personnel— teachers who provide related services and support to language learners, instructional coaches, and others—to better support the students and teachers at that grade level in an efficient manner. It also allows teams the option of intervening at Tier 1 as a grade level and makes it more likely that the grade-level team can access additional adult support during grade-level intervention time.

Table 2.2 (page 20) highlights conversation topics grade-level teams can have to support *all* students—including those who are special education eligible. A blueprint for teams to continue these conversations and ensure that all students have access to a guaranteed and viable curriculum is provided in chapter 4.

Table 2.2: Conversations and Activities for Grade-Level Teams

Topics	Potential Conversations and Activities
Student celebrations about learning	• How are we progressing toward our SMART goal?
Plans for upcoming instruction, including discussion about instructional strategies each teacher will use to teach to a target	• What are the upcoming learning targets? • What are students being asked to do? • What is the level of thinking required? • What are the essential elements of the standard or learning target? • Examine the unpacked standard, the scaffold, and the learning progression to determine the best instructional path for a special education student.
The development and administration of common assessments	• What assessment type is most appropriate for measuring mastery for each target? • Are there accommodations, modifications, or both that are appropriate for eligible students?
The discussion of formative data to drive instruction	• How many of our students have demonstrated mastery? • How many students need another boost? • Who are we really concerned about due to a pattern in the data? • Which students are ready to be extended?
Additional instructional design and planning in a cycle of instruction	• What are ideas for scaffolding and support?
Intervention design	• How will we differentiate in Tier 1 based on our data? • Will we intervene as a classroom teacher or a grade level (special education teacher included)? • Who will work with each group of students? • What are the best instructional strategies to use with each group?

The special education teacher is able to share a wide assortment of differentiation strategies that general education teachers benefit from greatly. Reciprocally, special education teachers may benefit from the ongoing, rich conversations about teaching and learning that happen between general educators.

Meghan Kennedy, a special education teacher in Kildeer Countryside Community Consolidated School District 96 who is responsible for grades 4 and 5 literacy and mathematics instruction as well as resource support, shared that the grades 4 and 5 teams at her school meet twice per week for one hour each time (M. Kennedy, personal communication, January 22, 2016). Due to the careful reconsideration of the master schedule by the school leadership team, she is able to attend one of those meetings for each grade level each week. In her role on the team, Meghan supports her colleagues in generating ideas and strategies in instructing struggling learners, in having conversations about text complexity and the use of a taxonomy, and in modifying materials when it is required due to individual student need. In turn, she gains a deep understanding of targets and about what her special education students need specifically when in her setting. Involvement in all grade-level activities, such as writing common formative assessments, allows Meghan to collaborate with grade-level team members and gain a clear understanding of what all students are expected to know and be able to do.

Reconsidering Building-Level Leadership Teams

Another elementary collaborative team structure includes building-level teams, such as a building-level leadership team. It is critical that any building-level leadership team not only include team leaders from each grade-level team but also a special education or related-services representative. This inclusion reinforces the concept that two separate and parallel systems of education (general education and special education) do not exist, but that one system exists for which all team members take collective responsibility. Table 2.3 lists conversations and activities the building-level leadership team participates in.

Table 2.3: Conversations and Activities for Building-Level Leadership Teams

Topics	Potential Conversations and Activities
Building-level problem solving	• What are team and school celebrations? • What timely learning conversations do we need to have at our next staff meeting? • How are we ensuring that all students are meaningful members of our school community?
Implementation of district and school initiatives and goals	• What is going well with implementations? • What are teams struggling with? • What do we need more clarity about? • How can we provide more clarity? • What resources do we need or what learning needs to happen to move us forward? • How are we progressing toward goals? • What do our data tell us?
Team-level communication	• What information do all team members need? • What input and feedback do we need to collect for our teams?

Building-level leadership teams that engage in these kinds of conversations develop into guiding coalitions that take collective ownership of all students' learning. Through deep dialogue and reflection on how to move teams forward, they ensure that they help build the capacity of all adults in the system through their own development as leaders.

Reconsidering Problem-Solving and Intervention Teams

The problem-solving or intervention team commonly includes special education teachers. This team addresses the need for a problem-solving process to be maintained when students receive special education services. Frequently monitoring special education data allows teams to adjust what is being done if it is not positively impacting a student's trend line, or data points over time. Teams should adjust intervention for special education students just as they would for general education students not making progress in a specific tier. Collaboratively examining the data on an ongoing basis also pushes teams to ensure that any underlying skill deficits or missing prerequisite skills related to a disability have been translated into an individualized education program (IEP) goal. Table 2.4 highlights these and other responsibilities the problem-solving and intervention team should discuss.

Table 2.4: Conversations and Activities for Problem-Solving and Intervention Teams

Topics	Potential Conversations and Activities
RTI implementation	• Assist in the development and implementation of a systematic pyramid of interventions. • Develop entry and exit criteria for tiers of intervention. • Document processes and protocols. • Communicate about the process. • Support grade-level teams in the process.
Improving building-level problem-solving processes	• Meet with grade-level teams to clarify the process. • Meet with grade-level teams to discuss and collaborate to address and support student needs. • Support teams in the referral process.
Monitoring students' progress	• Examine and analyze progress-monitoring data of students in tiers of intervention. • Use data to move students through the intervention tiers. • Analyze the progress-monitoring data of special education–eligible students with the case manager. • Collaborate on the adjustment of goals based on progress. • Examine the existing skill deficits of special education students to ensure missing prerequisite skills translate into IEP goals.

Problem-solving and intervention teams share responsibility for ensuring that all educators understand and put in place clear criteria for inclusion in identified interventions. They are also important liaisons supporting teams in brainstorming effective strategies for students who struggle and in assisting in data collection that might be necessary in order to identify next steps. Members of problem-solving or intervention teams suggest strategies that are effective for *all* students, not just those who have or are suspected of having a disability. These teams must hold the system accountable for the continuation of a data-based problem-solving process even after special education eligibility exists.

Reconsidering Job-Alike, Cross-School Teams

Lastly, many schools have (and we recommend) a job-alike, cross-school team structure. This team structure can be powerful, particularly related to broader curricular teaching and learning initiatives. This team may include a teacher representative from each content area and grade-level team at an elementary school, across a district, or both. For instance, if there were three members of a third-grade team at one elementary school, one of those teachers may be the representative to literacy; one to mathematics; and one to science, social studies, or both of these subjects. In a system that includes multiple elementary, middle, or high schools, these representatives come from schools across the district. In a system with only one school at each level, those representatives may meet vertically (with the literacy representative from the grade level above or below). We also strongly recommend developing a collaborative relationship with a neighboring school district, as cross-school collaboration provides a powerful opportunity to step outside of your daily context and to stretch your thinking around teaching and learning. Electronic teams also present opportunities for job-alike collaboration. It is critical that special education teachers are included in a job-alike structure in the area for which they have core content responsibilities. A job-alike team may engage in conversations and tasks such as those table 2.5 (page 24) provides.

When content-alike teachers discuss priority or power standards, unpack them to identify targets, and pace them throughout the school year, special educators must be included in the conversations. As part of the team, they gain a better understanding of what mastery looks like and the level of rigor a target requires. This deepens content knowledge and allows professionals to benefit from the wisdom of the collective *we*.

Table 2.5: Conversations and Activities for Job-Alike, Cross-School Teams

Topics	Potential Conversations and Activities
Unpacking the standards and working to identify power or priority standards	• What are the components of the standard? • What level of rigor is involved? • How would we know if students could meet this expectation? • What is a logical learning progression? • Discuss scaffolding ideas for students struggling to meet the standard. • Identify the key things that need to happen for a student to be able to master the learning targets.
Creating pacing guides or scope and sequence	• How much instructional time is necessary for in-depth instruction that includes intervening? • Consider time-of-year issues (timing of accountability assessments, and so on). • Consider connections to other targets. • Consider instructional implications in the use of resources.
Developing benchmark assessments	• Based on benchmark results, what can we predict about how our students will do on external accountability assessments since our standards are aligned? • What accommodations, modifications, or both need to be addressed for eligible students? • Ensure that what is being taught is what is being assessed.
Selecting materials	• Review newly published curricular materials for standards alignment. • Make recommendations regarding resources.
Subject-specific data analysis	• As a district, what are our greatest areas of vulnerability in literacy, mathematics, science, and other subjects? • What are we doing well as a system?

Working Together in Secondary Teams

Secondary structures can be very similar in nature and require the same participation level from special educators. Table 2.6 illustrates some common secondary team structures.

At the secondary level, however, it becomes more of a challenge to ensure that teams are meaningful with specific and purposeful work to do due to the departmental nature of traditional junior high and middle schools and high schools. Two different

Table 2.6: Potential Secondary Teams

	Cross-Curricular Teams	Content-Alike Teams	Job-Alike, Cross-School Teams
Who	*All* content-area teachers working with the same team of students (middle school model or school-within-a-school model)	*All* teachers of the same content across teams within the building	*All* teachers of the same content across the district or across multiple schools
Focus	• Students (celebration and problem solving) • Planning (logistics, cross content skills–based connections) • Skills across content areas	• Common assessments • Data analysis • Instructional design and planning	• Power standards • Pacing guides • Benchmark assessments • Materials selection • Instructional design and planning • Data analysis
Frequency	• Twice per week during common planning time in middle school • Less frequently as high school skills–based teams	• One to two times per week during common planning time • During staff meetings	• Monthly

secondary teams might include one made up of teachers who teach the same course (such as an algebra 1 team) and another made up of a content department (such as a mathematics department team). The work to be done in these two teams should be different and clearly identified.

Reconsidering Cross-Curricular Teams

One of the more common purposes of a secondary cross-curricular team is to identify skills that have been deemed to be areas of need based on data for a given school. Cross-curricular teams develop how those skills will be taught and assessed across content areas. One high school cross-curricular team identifies how each subject area and course would apply a collaboratively developed writing rubric to ensure that teachers across content areas are using like vocabulary, using the same rubric for assessment, and giving consistent feedback on writing that has been identified as an area of need in the team's school. This cross-curricular collaboration focuses on schoolwide data, rallies teachers around a common need, and reinforces that students' learning is a collective responsibility. Including special educators on teams underscores the beliefs that all students can learn at high levels and that all educators are accountable for each student's success. Lisa Ruff, a special education teacher at Twin Groves Middle School in Buffalo Grove, Illinois, describes the evolution of her participation on collaborative teams:

> Prior to working in a professional learning community environment, special education was an island on its own. Once special education was included in team-level meetings, we were able to meet on a daily basis. I also have access to all of the clinicians that support my students. So what used to happen is that people would say, "Well it's OK that they didn't learn," because they are special ed and have this gap. The new, more collaborative environment has made it not okay [to say that]. We are all accountable for these students' learning. We teach to the regular grade-level targets to ensure all students have the same core skills. All of us being accountable are what closes the gap, and that's what we want for all of our students. (L. Ruff, personal communication, April 2013)

Collaboration on content targets is just as essential at the secondary level as it is at the elementary level. Given that co-teaching is on the rise in secondary schools, collective conversations about content targets, mastery, and assessment are even more critical. Equal partnership between special and general educators in the understanding and delivery of content avoids the risk of special education co-teachers becoming glorified aides.

Reconsidering Content-Alike Teams

Content-alike teams at the secondary level function similarly to the grade-level teams at the elementary level. Teachers who teach the same course have dedicated time to consider and respond collectively to the questions and activities in table 2.2 (page 20). While both elementary and secondary content-alike teams discuss interventions and instructional strategies, collectively planning for intervention differs between the two since it is less likely that secondary content-alike teams have the opportunity to intervene collectively. Secondary master schedules rarely are able to accommodate multiple sections of the same course scheduled parallel to each other. However, building content-specific intervention time into the schedule makes collective interventions possible.

Unfortunately, special educators who teach the content either in a co-teaching model or in a special education instructional setting are often excluded from content-alike teams. If we are going to commit to keeping students on appropriate grade-level targets, including special educators on these teams is a necessity. Conversations focused on what mastery looks like and the learning progressions that lead to mastery cannot exclude any teacher who teaches the content. While the logistics of including both special and general educators on content-alike teams pose a challenge, they are not a valid excuse. Recognizing the potential number of a secondary special education teacher's course preps heightens the urgency to develop a shared responsibility for all students' learning and makes clear communication between general and special educators paramount. Secondary teams that we have worked with across the United States indicate that highly collaborative, content-alike teams that have deep conversations focused on student learning and sharing strategies broaden the collective effectiveness of their members.

Reconsidering Job-Alike, Cross-School Teams

At the secondary level, job-alike teams include all teachers who teach a specific course, and cross-school teams include all teachers who teach a specific course across schools in a larger district. In these team structures at the secondary level, questions and activities mirror the questions and activities posed in table 2.5 (page 24). The work at this level is further away from day-to-day classroom activities. Instead, it focuses on a guaranteed and viable curriculum across classrooms and schools and on more summative pieces of assessment that provide systemwide data to allow for calibration of the curriculum.

In smaller systems where there is a single school that serves particular grade levels, we highly recommend developing a cross-school collaborative opportunity with another school in your area though it may be part of a different school district. As authors, we believe it is powerful to step outside of your own context periodically to have professional conversations about student learning. Teams in this structure may collaborate face-to-face or electronically via a digital environment.

Fusing Collaboration and Professional Development

When there is collective responsibility for all students' learning, it is difficult to understand why special educators are often not part of the professional development plan provided for teachers. When reading teachers participate in sessions on research-based literacy practices, special education teachers who teach literacy are often grouped together to work on tasks related to procedural safeguards unrelated to good instruction. This is commonly the case across content areas.

The deep work that the chapters in part II outline, combined with the work that happens on an ongoing basis in collaborative teams, will lead to consistent and meaningful improvement over time. So when systems struggle with the logistics of ensuring that teachers who teach our most vulnerable students be included in ongoing, high-quality professional development, the question that we should really be asking ourselves is, "How is it that this does not happen universally in all school systems?" We cannot afford the irresponsibility of excluding those who teach our most at-risk students from all high-quality professional development focused on best practices. We encourage you to ask yourselves, "Does collaboratively doing this work improve teaching and thus student learning?" If the answer is *yes* and special educators are not at the table, then the question really becomes, "Does *all* really mean *all*?"

Yes We Can: Keys to Moving Forward

Collaborative teams may take many forms, but regardless of their structure, they must include both general and special educators to support all students' learning.

- Consider current collaborative team structures, and examine whether:
  - The work of each team is clearly identified and feasible
  - The membership of the team is inclusive of *all* who teach and support the content
  - Adequate time is allocated for each team to address the questions and activities appropriate to the role of the team
  - Team structures allow for collaboration outside the daily context of your single school
- Identify a meaningful focus for cross-content teams based on student learning.
- Identify how collaboration between general and special educators will be a mutual responsibility.

Educators must commit to a shared responsibility to ensure all students learn. Chapter 3 outlines action steps that teachers can take to put this commitment into action and ensure a guaranteed and viable curriculum for all students.

CHAPTER 3

DEVELOPING A CULTURE OF SHARED LEARNING EXPECTATIONS

One of the most significant factors that impacts student achievement is that teachers commit to implementing a guaranteed and viable curriculum to ensure no matter who teaches a given class, the curriculum will address certain essential content.

—Robert J. Marzano

It is essential for all students to have access to a guaranteed and viable curriculum (Marzano, 2003; Saphier, 2005). A clear understanding of this concept is critical for its true implementation. *Guaranteed,* simply put, means that all students, regardless of teacher, eligibility, or status, will have access to the same standards, understandings, content, and skills across a school and system. All teachers have a unique style that, in the highest-performing classrooms, they adapt to meet the needs of the learners. While it is not essential that teachers instruct in the same way, all staff must focus on the same learning expectations for students during instruction and through assessment. *Viable* signifies that the curriculum must be doable within the time frame provided. When a curriculum is not viable, teachers feel they must cover content rather than help learners truly demonstrate mastery. In turn, students are not able to focus on deeply understanding the essential content. This is a careful consideration, as all states have assessments to which they are accountable; therefore, pacing must also allow for student success on these annual measures. Creating a guaranteed and viable curriculum relies on teams' collaboration in deciding grade-level and course expectations, content pacing, and assessment practices and on their regular review of performance data to make informed instructional decisions.

Saphier (2005) expands on the concepts of guaranteed and viable curriculum, outlining "an academic focus that begins with a set of practices that bring clarity, coherence, and precision to every teacher's classroom work" (as cited in DuFour et al., 2010, p. 71). Citing Saphier's (2005) work, DuFour and colleagues (2010) reiterate that "teachers work collaboratively to provide a rigorous curriculum" that all members of the teaching team agree on and understand and that "includes a compact list of learning expectations for each grade or course, and that provides tangible exemplars of student proficiency for each learning expectation" (p. 71).

Based on our collective experience, we maintain that clearly answering PLC critical question 1, What is it we expect our students to learn?, is the first step and one of the most powerful steps to improving outcomes for students with special needs, and it begins to provide the foundation for establishing a guaranteed and viable curriculum. Looking at a typical high school special education resource teacher's caseload, for example, it is easy to see why answering this critical question is essential to creating comprehensive team support for students with special needs. Because mainstream teachers traditionally establish their own curricular priorities, implement their own individual grading practices, and assess students using their preferred methods, the weight given to things like homework, participation, and assessments can vary greatly and be a significant factor in success. In other words, what is required and expected for success is different from teacher to teacher. A resource teacher working with seven or eight students from different classrooms may thus have multiple sets of prioritized standards, assessments, and curricular content to navigate. Taking time to understand each general education teacher's individual practices is time spent away from helping students master targets. Unfortunately, situations where special educators must address gaps in general education teachers' practices are all too common, and they are disastrous both for the special education teacher and for students. Such practices highlight the way clearly defined learning targets can help improve instruction and communication between mainstream and special education teachers.

So how can systems truly implement a guaranteed and viable curriculum for students? In his report on levels of school effectiveness, Marzano (2012) identifies six essential indicators of a guaranteed and viable curriculum.

1. "The school curriculum and accompanying assessments adhere to state and district standards" (p. 10).

2. "The school curriculum is focused enough that it can be adequately addressed in the time available to teachers" (p. 10).

3. "All students have the opportunity to learn the critical content of the curriculum" (p. 11).

4. "Clear and measurable goals are established and focused on critical needs regarding improving overall student achievement at the school level" (p. 11).

5. "Data are analyzed, interpreted, and used to regularly monitor progress toward school achievement goals" (p. 12).

6. "Appropriate school-level and classroom-level processes and practices are in place to help students meet individual achievement goals when data indicate interventions are needed" (p. 12).

All this makes sense, but let's consider what these indicators look like when they are (or are not) put to use in our schools, and specifically how they apply to special education. Table 3.1 explains the evidence that shows these six indicators meet the needs of diverse learners and support special educators.

Table 3.1: Six Indicators of a Guaranteed and Viable Curriculum

Indicator	Absent When . . .	Present When . . .
The school curriculum and accompanying assessments adhere to state and district standards.	• Locally developed curriculum is not aligned to standards. • Classroom instruction is inconsistently aligned to standards or agreed-on priorities.	• Alignment is evident among state standards, local standards, local curriculum, grade-level and content-area pacing guides, team assessments, *and* classroom instruction.
The school curriculum is focused enough that it can be adequately addressed in the time available to teachers.	• Focus is on coverage of content, not mastery of content. • Less than 80 percent of students demonstrate proficiency on identified standards. • Intervention systems are overwhelmed. • Teachers experience burnout. • Students are stressed out. • There is a lack of clear understanding of and consistency about priorities in the curriculum.	• Pacing guides drive instruction within established time parameters consistently across classrooms and schools. • Priority standards are identified and are a focus for instruction. • Assessments align to priority standards to inform instruction and reporting.

continued →

Indicator	Absent When . . .	Present When . . .
All students have the opportunity to learn the critical content of the curriculum.	• Students with special needs are exposed to less rigorous standards than typical peers. • Students with special needs are exposed to fewer standards than typical peers. • Students with special needs are exposed to different standards than typical peers.	• Students with special needs are expected to master grade-level and course standards and are provided time, support, and resources to do so. • Special educators are an integral part of the grade-level or course collaborative team. • Students with special needs are exposed to rigorous texts. • Special educators participate in professional development about instructional practices alongside their general education peers.
Clear and measurable goals are established and focused on critical needs for improving overall student achievement at the school level.	• Practices are inconsistent across classrooms. • Instruction, assessment, and reporting vary from teacher to teacher. • A school, team, or both have absent or unclear goals. • There is a lack of focus on student-achievement data. • Data of students with special needs are absent in the data review and SMART goal process.	• Consistent instruction, assessment, and reporting practices are developed and discussed collaboratively. • IEP goals align to standards and target areas of deficit. • Accommodations are purposefully identified and utilized to help students access the curriculum; modifications are made sparingly.
Data are analyzed, interpreted, and used to regularly monitor progress toward school achievement goals.	• Data-analysis protocols are absent or ineffective. • Individual teachers examine their data; teams and the school do not. • Short-cycle review of progress-monitoring data is absent after special education eligibility is determined.	• Data drive instruction for all learners. • Additional time, support, and resources are provided for all students as needed. • Problem-solving processes continue after special education eligibility.

Indicator	Absent When . . .	Present When . . .
Appropriate school-level and classroom-level processes and practices are in place to help students meet individual achievement goals when data indicate interventions are needed.	• Curriculum is implemented inconsistently. • Resources are selected by individual teachers. • Intervention systems are haphazard and without clear criteria for entry, exit, or both.	• Research-based programming and best practices in instructional methodology are implemented at Tiers 1, 2, and 3. • Tier 1 intervention is aligned to priority standards. • Tier 2 and Tier 3 interventions are driven by diagnostic assessments to identify specific needs and implemented with fidelity.

Source: Adapted from Marzano, 2012.

Please note these beliefs apply to the vast majority of learners in the education system, special education entitled or not. When we consider students with significant cognitive impairments, we must, of course, approach these concepts with a slightly different perspective. We'll speak further to that point later in this chapter.

Establishing a School Culture That Supports All Students

We know that special education services are most effective when they:

- Are delivered in the general education setting to the maximum extent possible

- Are targeted to fill gaps between a student's disability and the demands of the setting

- Ensure the same opportunities to achieve high standards regardless of setting

But how do we build school cultures to accomplish all this? Simply put, we have to make some pivotal shifts. Table 3.2 (page 34) summarizes the schoolwide cultural shifts needed to support all learners.

In the absence of these shifts, educators will continue to perpetuate a belief system that presumes most students—not *all* students—can learn. If educators truly believe that all students can and will learn, then they must work to shift our culture to act in the same ways. These shifts demand teachers focus on each learner as a unique individual. Whether schools or districts are grappling with implementation of the CCSS or another set of state or national standards, they all must consider the importance of preparing students for their futures in college, careers, and beyond.

Table 3.2: Schoolwide Cultural Shifts Necessary to Support All Learners

From	To
A focus on teaching	A focus on learning
An emphasis on what was taught	A fixation on what was learned
Coverage of content	Demonstration of proficiency
Private practice	Open sharing of practice
Individual responsibility	Collective responsibility
Each teacher assigning priority to different learning standards	Collaborative teams determining the priority of standards

Source: DuFour et al., 2010.

Sadly, educators often doubt students with special needs' ability to meet these rigorous expectations. Our response as authors to such reservations is simple: *all* means *all*, with the understanding that educators may have to tailor instruction by providing scaffolds, accommodations, and modifications to ensure that all students are successful.

Instructionally, then, educators must first answer a fundamental question when considering, "Does *all* mean *all*?" That question is, "Will this student ever be expected to function independently when he or she leaves the public school system?" (Buffum, Mattos, & Weber, 2009). As we outline in the following sections, answers to that question dictate at least two possible courses of action.

When Students Are Expected to Function Independently

Teachers have a moral obligation to make every effort to get students to proficiency. They cannot modify the standards students are expected to reach. Educators must include the vast majority of students and most eligibility categories in the goal to attain proficiency in the general curriculum. In fact, "Students with special needs must be challenged to excel within the general curriculum and be prepared for success in their postschool lives, including college or careers" (NGA & CCSSO, n.d.b, p. 1). More rigorous standards provide students with special needs with the opportunity to access rigorous academic content. In reaching this diverse student group, "how these high standards are taught and assessed is of the utmost importance" (NGA & CCSSO, n.d.b, p. 1). When educators continuously develop their understanding of "research-based instructional practices and focus on their effective implementation, they help improve access to mathematics and English language arts (ELA) standards for all students," including those with special needs (Massachusetts Department of

Elementary and Secondary Education, 2011, p. 99). In order for students with special needs "to meet high academic standards and to fully demonstrate their conceptual and procedural knowledge and skills . . . instruction must also incorporate supports and accommodations" specific to each learner's profile (NGA & CCSSO, n.d.b, p. 1).

When Students Are *Not* Expected to Function Independently

Teams must rephrase the critical questions to state, What do we want *this* student to know and be able to do? How will we know if he or she learns it? Such students will likely be working toward modified standards, but the work they must do remains standards aligned, purposefully scaffolded to increase rigor, and formatively assessed to provide feedback as well as to drive instructional adjustment.

Teams collaborate in regard to the expectations for each individual learner so that their efforts merge into a cohesive support plan and maintain a results orientation based on the individual student's growth and progress. Collaboration is specific to functional curriculum implementation; that is to say, it is specific to the curriculum being taught. Teachers who support students with disabilities that rarely occur in terms of complexity or impact—what we call *low-incidence conditions*—collaborate with other teachers working with the same type of population to share best practices. Together, teachers and staff form a collaborative team and create a strategic plan for their collaboration, setting expectations for how (such as in person or electronically) and when they will regularly work collaboratively. For example, two elementary schools in two different Illinois school districts, Kildeer Countryside Community Consolidated School District 96 and Mannheim School District 83, created a partnership for their low-incidence program teachers. In the separate districts, collaboration was difficult due to the limited number of classrooms and, therefore, staff in place for students with significant needs. These two schools worked together to establish monthly conference calls with shared agendas in order to support each other, explore resources, problem solve, celebrate successes, and learn together. As these colleagues built both relationships and shared knowledge, their connections became even more deeply rooted and organic. Teachers and related-services providers in one school visited the sister school in order to see the environment and meet face-to-face with their colleagues. Teams from both schools found that collaborating with each other in person was incredibly powerful, particularly since they had invested so much time in sharing practices prior to the visits.

In fact, when teachers share their best practices, they affirm the goal of working collaboratively to ensure that all students learn at high levels. While the learning targets may look different from shared grade-level standards in order to meet the needs of individual students with significant special needs, teams still work to answer the four critical questions for that student. In these considerations for students who are not expected to function independently, it is important to remember that:

> Some students with the most significant cognitive disabilities will require substantial supports and accommodations to have meaningful access to certain standards in both instruction and assessment, based on their communication and academic needs. These supports and accommodations should ensure that students receive access to multiple means of learning and opportunities to demonstrate knowledge. (NGA & CCSSO, n.d.b, p. 2)

The team of teachers and related-services providers (speech pathologists, psychologists, occupational therapists, physical therapists, and others) forms its own collaborative team, targeting each student's growth. Through the lens of the PLC questions that lead to high levels of learning for *all* students, collaborative teams provide the substantial supports these students need to learn and to demonstrate their knowledge.

Ensuring That All Students Learn at High Levels

Even for students with the most significant impairments, the expectation that learners can and will make progress is still very much in effect. Maintaining a growth mindset is essential. Students can and will do what educators believe they can do; if they put limits on students' abilities and potential, they essentially *guarantee* that those limits become learners' maximum potential. Therefore, it is the responsibility of every educator working with every student to put in place the conditions and beliefs that he or she can, and will, learn at high levels.

How do educators create the conditions where there are no limits put on student learning? The first and most important element to have in place is a guaranteed and viable curriculum. Without it, we leave curriculum access to teacher discretion, and therefore, student progress becomes unpredictable. When we recall our own days as students, we can probably remember anxiously awaiting the arrival of our schedules because we knew our assigned teachers would determine what our experience would be. Those of us in education who have our own children in school commonly wander into the counselor's or principal's office to discuss teachers who may best fit our own children's needs. Some may consider this access a perk of the profession. Those outside education may call it insider trading. We have inside information about what the outcomes may be for each teacher's students. We have to ask ourselves whether it is okay that outcomes from teacher to teacher may vary widely. Shouldn't there be some guarantees as to what students will be exposed to and learn? Shouldn't there be some consistency in the level of support they will receive when they aren't learning? Educators must agree that accepting such inconsistencies simply cannot continue, particularly in light of the data presented about teachers' abilities to close the gap for students with special needs.

Yes We Can: Keys to Moving Forward

When general and special educators work together in collaborative teams to ensure a guaranteed and viable curriculum for all students, they model their commitment and belief that all students can learn. As you work with your team, consider the following keys to moving forward.

- Focus all collaborative teamwork on answering the four critical PLC questions as they relate to the grade-level standards.

- For students whose needs are so complex that the grade-level standards are not attainable, focus all collaborative teamwork on answering the four critical PLC questions as they relate to moving that student closer to functional access to the grade-level standards.

- Question mindset constantly: do we, as a team, really believe that *all* means *all*?

In part II, we examine how collaborative teams within PLCs can close the achievement gap by focusing on learning and results. Chapter 4 asks general and special educators to consider what they want students to know and be able to do. We provide a tool for unpacking standards to help guide teams as they answer this critical question.

PART II

Closing the Gap Through a Focus on Learning and Results

CHAPTER 4

ESTABLISHING WHAT ALL STUDENTS SHOULD LEARN

Implementing a strategy of common, rigorous standards with differentiated resources and instruction can create excellence and equity for all students.

—Stacey M. Childress, Denis P. Doyle,
and David A. Thomas

When general educators and special educators work together to develop a shared understanding of learning expectations, all students benefit from their collective wisdom. Educators learn from and with each other as they consider the road map to focused, consistent teaching and learning, beginning with asking and answering the first critical question for PLC teams, What is it we expect our students to learn? This question can be answered in a variety of ways by teacher teams and individuals in a system. Some may present the state standards and say, "This is the answer to critical question 1; we are good to go." Unfortunately, without careful consideration of the standards, each teacher may prioritize, interpret, and apply the standards differently. Others may say, "We have our textbook and it defines what students should know and be able to do, so we don't need to think about this." We all know the flaws in this thinking. For one, it is nearly impossible to teach an entire textbook cover to cover in one school year, and we can't be sure there is consistency in teachers' interpretations of what is prioritized in the textbook. There may even be some who say, "I have taught ancient civilizations for the past twenty years, and the topics I have taught have worked for me and are what I believe students should know and be able to do in my classroom." Special educators likely have their own set of expectations based on what they believe their students are capable of mastering.

The sheer number of ways educators may respond to PLC critical question 1 leads to marked differences in teaching and learning for those teaching the same grade level, subject area, or course. Let's take a look at two sixth-grade students' experiences in the same middle school, where faculty rely on curriculum guides in textbooks to provide the answer to the question, What is it we expect our students to learn?

- **Case 1:** Joey has Mr. Smith for social studies, and Mr. Smith loves to teach ancient Egypt. He spends twelve weeks, on what is supposed to be a three-week unit, teaching ancient Egypt because he truly believes there is a lot to learn from that world, and he loves many of the fun activities he has taught for years. It is difficult for him to imagine students leaving sixth grade without mummifying a chicken or creating models of the pyramids. Mr. Smith realizes that he might have to skim through ancient Greece and other civilizations to complete all these activities, but he is really okay with that.

- **Case 2:** Lisa has Mrs. Johnson for sixth-grade social studies. Mrs. Johnson believes that it is important for students to learn about all the ancient civilizations outlined in the textbook. She paces instruction to be sure that students have a clear understanding of how all ancient civilizations shaped the world today.

Joey and Lisa have had very different experiences in social studies, so we can't really be sure what knowledge and skills they have mastered entering seventh grade. According to Mike Schmoker and Robert J. Marzano (1999), this creates *curriculum chaos*—every teacher making these decisions in isolation based on what he or she feels is most important. What students must learn is based on individual teachers' preferences instead of on an agreed-on set of learning outcomes.

Eliminating Curriculum Chaos and Taking Action

Special educators and others who provide support to students with special needs have to navigate scenarios like Joey's and Lisa's experiences, oftentimes in many subject areas, for their caseload of students. A special educator trying to scaffold support for students must first examine each teacher's expected course outcomes and then determine the best way to approach support. Commonly agreed-on learning targets not only benefit students with special needs and make it easier for special educators to support students (although that should have some weight), but they also establish a collective understanding about what is important for students to know and be able to do for all students in a grade level, subject, course, or all the above. Clear learning targets, collaboration among teachers, and a guaranteed and viable curriculum send students to the next level of learning with common knowledge of concepts and skills. To ensure a guaranteed and viable curriculum, we must carefully attend to PLC critical question 1. The processes defined in this chapter provide a course of action for answering this question.

While we recommend that the practice of prioritizing and unpacking standards ideally happens at the school or district level, this chapter offers three action steps teacher teams—including special educators who teach the same grade level, subject area, or course—can take immediately. The intention is for teams to focus more on learning and learning expectations and less on teaching, moving closer to a guaranteed and viable curriculum without having to wait for the school or district to embark on this effort. When special educators participate as equal partners alongside their general curriculum peers in these three action steps, all students and teachers benefit. Special educators can secure more support for students in meeting their IEP goals and grade-level expectations. The ideas in this chapter can be adapted and applied to a larger-scale implementation for schools or districts that are ready to get started, but this may require further considerations that are not outlined. For more detailed information about implementing this work at the school or district level, please see *Common Formative Assessment: A Toolkit for Professional Learning Communities at Work* (Bailey & Jakicic, 2012); for the process as it specifically relates to the CCSS, try *Collaborating for Success With the Common Core: A Toolkit for Professional Learning Communities at Work* (Bailey, Jakicic, & Spiller, 2014).

The action steps outlined are based on the premise that the work will be done collaboratively. When referencing teams in the action steps, we are referring to elementary grade-level teams or middle or high school content- or course-specific teams. In small school districts, it is likely that there are singletons, or one teacher per grade level or course. In this scenario, we recommend virtual collaboration with other small schools, or vertical teams where collaboration occurs across grade levels by content area or course. Most important, it is imperative that the team includes special educators working alongside general educators.

Let's consider three action steps for teams to take toward establishing a guaranteed and viable curriculum that outlines clear expectations for what students will learn: (1) select an upcoming unit or topic and decide what students should know and be able to do, (2) prioritize the list of what students should know and be able to do, and (3) unpack the priority standards.

Selecting an Upcoming Unit or Topic and Deciding What Students Should Know and Be Able to Do

Brainstorm everything students should know and be able to do as a result of instruction for the unit or topic. Be prepared to have any documents that will help focus the conversation at the team's disposal during this brainstorming step. These may include things like curriculum maps, pacing guides, state standards, teacher textbook resources, standards-based report cards, and so on.

It is important for teams to remember that they are not making decisions yet regarding what will be prioritized and what will not; they are simply creating a list. We do not mean a list of teacher actions that will take place during the unit or a list of activities or projects students will participate in. Instead, the list should include the state, local, or other learning targets that will be met as a result of the unit or topic focus. It is easy to get caught up in listing all the activities that will take place during the unit in this step, but remember to keep the focus on the learning that will take place, not what students will do. The following English language arts and science examples are considered activities, not learning standards or targets.

- **English language arts:** Underline the textual evidence that supports the theme of a story.

- **Science:** Create a model of the solar system.

Both activities facilitate students' understanding and mastery of the learning target, but they are not learning targets.

The learning targets for these activities could include the following.

- **English language arts:** Cite textual evidence to support understanding of how evidence supports designation of a theme (NGA & CCSSO, 2010a).

- **Science:** Demonstrate that Earth is one of eight planets varying in size, structure, appearance, and distance from the sun the planet orbits.

The learning targets define what it is students should know and be able to do at the end of learning. They do not define the projects, assignments, or assessments that will take place to facilitate and measure learning.

If there is a shared list of standards that generally guide teaching and learning for each subject or course in your school and teachers are familiar with the standards, this process should be fairly easy for teams to complete. The process of identifying a list of learning targets for a unit or topic of focus may be more difficult if standards-based instruction is not currently the focus of teaching and learning. In this case, we suggest that the team spend time familiarizing itself with the state or local standards first and then begin to align standards to the unit of instruction. In order to decide what standards document to become familiar with, the team should work with school or district administration to determine expectations for standards alignment. For example, a school or district may determine that the state standards indicate what every student should know and be able to do, or it may have a set of local standards that guide teaching and learning. If it is still unclear after discussions with school or district administration, we recommend focusing on the state standards since they are likely what will be addressed on the state assessment. This step can be skipped if the team already has a shared list of what students should know and be able to do as a result of the unit or topic. In this case, the team can move directly to action step 2.

Prioritizing the List of What Students Should Know and Be Able to Do

The brainstormed list's length depends on the unit or topic's depth and length. If teams discover that the list includes only one or two learning standards but the unit takes ten weeks, the team should discuss the unit length and determine whether it is appropriate. The standards' rigor and complexity may be contributing to the unit length, or it may be that students are engaged in a large number of activities during the unit. In the latter case, an examination of the activities and their value in helping students master the learning standards is in order.

If the list of standards is long, the team should consider prioritizing the standards to determine which ones it believes all students must learn before leaving that grade level, subject area, or course. This does not mean that the team will eliminate the other standards identified; rather, it simply means that the prioritized standards will be emphasized most during instruction, will be assessed more formally by the team, and will be those for which it will provide additional time and support when students struggle to learn them (Bailey & Jakicic, 2012).

We suggest that teams use the "Simple as 1, 2, 3" prioritizing process in appendix A (pages 110–111) for determining priority standards. In this process, teams will follow three steps.

1. Individual team members use set criteria to make initial choices about which standards to prioritize.

2. As a team, team members discuss their selections and develop an initial list of priority standards.

3. Finally, they take other sources of information, such as standards from subsequent grade levels and data from accountability assessments, into consideration to guide their final decision about which standards to prioritize.

The next section outlines these steps in greater detail, which illustrates the important points to remember in the process, identifies the materials necessary, and explains the steps.

Once teams complete this process and compile their final list of priority standards, it is time to unpack the standards to determine and examine more closely the expectations each learning standard holds about what students need to know and be able to do.

Unpacking the Priority Standards

The critical process of unpacking standards involves breaking the standard into smaller components to gain a deep understanding of the expectations packed into each. When teams or even individual teachers unpack a standard, they engage in a process that assists them in developing instructional plans and assessments that lead to better, more focused instruction and, ultimately, higher levels of learning for more students. They can even pinpoint the areas where students may struggle and plan ahead for scaffolded supports. Unpacking standards enables every teacher who teaches the standard to develop a deep and consistent understanding of the standard and its component expectations. The outcome is that students will receive instruction that is truly aligned to the expected rigor and complexity of the standard. A special educator we have had the opportunity to work with described the process of unpacking the standards as eye-opening. She explained that before she participated in the unpacking process with her general education colleagues, she had made inaccurate assumptions about standards' expectations. Her sixth-grade students were expected to demonstrate proficiency on the Common Core Reading standard RL.6.2: "Determine a theme or central idea of a text and how it is conveyed through particular details; provide a summary of the text distinct from personal opinions or judgments" (NGA & CCSSO, 2010a). Without the benefit of a team discussion regarding the expectations embedded in this standard, she modified it for her students, asking them to simply identify a theme or central idea of a text and list details from the text that supported the theme. She also considered the summary of the text as a separate component and did not connect theme, details, and summary in her instruction or assessment. Later, when she joined the grade-level team at its weekly collaborative meetings, the team's discussion of this standard helped her realize that students were expected to show that they could integrate how a theme is conveyed using the details in an objective summary of the text. She realized that she was expecting a lot less of her students than the general education teachers were and that she needed to focus on the scaffolds and supports students would need to ensure that they could meet the more rigorous expectations. As this example shows, this process is particularly valuable for special educators as they determine the best way to navigate learning for students with varying special needs.

Bailey and Jakicic (2012) describe unpacking as a strategy that enables collaborative teams "to achieve collective clarity and agreement regarding specific *learning targets* contained within the standards" (p. 79). They further define learning targets as the increments of learning—steps of knowledge or concepts and skills—that build on each other and culminate in attainment of the standard.

Using the protocol in figure 4.1, teams follow a seven-step process to unpack their prioritized standards into learning targets: (1) identify the priority standards, (2) identify the verbs (skills) and knowledge (concepts), (3) identify learning targets, (4) determine the level of rigor and examine assessment types, (5) identify key vocabulary, (6) determine a logical learning progression, and (7) determine potential scaffolds and supports. (See appendix A, page 112, for a free reproducible version of this figure.)

Standards:				
What Will Students Do (Skills or Verbs)	**With What Knowledge or Concept**	**Level of Thinking or Type of Assessment**	**Vocabulary**	**Scaffolds or Supports**
Learning Progression:				

Figure 4.1: Protocol for unpacking standards.

In our discussion of the seven-step unpacking process, we use the following standard from the Common Core mathematics grade 6 standards to illustrate the protocol so that teams can follow the process from start to finish (NGA & CCSSO, 2010b):

> 6.RP.A.3—Use ratio and rate reasoning to solve real-world and mathematical problems, e.g., by reasoning about tables of equivalent ratios, tape diagrams, double number line diagrams, or equations.

Additionally, we provide a complete example using two Common Core English language arts standards for grade 6 at the end of this chapter (see figure 4.9, pages 60–61).

Step 1: Identify the Priority Standards

Teams will insert one or more standards for a particular unit or topic of instruction into the first row of the protocol for unpacking standards (figure 4.2, page 48).

Standard: 6.RP.A.3—Use ratio and rate reasoning to solve real-world and mathematical problems, such as by reasoning about tables of equivalent ratios, tape diagrams, double number line diagrams, or equations.

What Will Students Do (Skills or Verbs)	With What Knowledge or Concept	Level of Thinking or Type of Assessment	Vocabulary	Scaffolds or Supports

Learning Progression:

Source for standard: NGA & CCSSO, 2010b.

Figure 4.2: Example of unpacking process step 1.

Each priority standard in the unit will be unpacked either in combination with another standard or on its own. Teams can insert more than one standard at a time into the unpacking document if standards will be integrated during instruction. For instance, instruction for the following two Common Core mathematics standards would likely be integrated. Because students would need to know that numbers that are not rational are called *irrational* and would need to understand decimal expansion in order to use rational approximations of irrational numbers to compare the size of irrational numbers, locate them on a number line, and estimate the value of expressions, collaborative team members may want to unpack these standards together (NGA & CCSSO, 2010b):

8.NS.A.1—Know that numbers that are not rational are called irrational. Understand informally that every number has a decimal expansion; for rational numbers show that the decimal expansion repeats eventually, and convert a decimal expansion which repeats eventually into a rational number.

8.NS.A.2—Use rational approximations of irrational numbers to compare the size of irrational numbers, locate them approximately on a number line diagram, and estimate the value of expressions (e.g., π^2).

Step 2: Identify Verbs (Skills) and Knowledge (Concepts)

Teams will circle or highlight the verbs and underline the knowledge and concepts students will perform or demonstrate through those actions (figure 4.3).

Standard: 6.RP.A.3—Use ratio and rate reasoning to solve real-world and mathematical problems, such as by reasoning about tables of equivalent ratios, tape diagrams, double number line diagrams, or equations.				
What Will Students Do (Skills or Verbs)	**With What Knowledge or Concept**	**Level of Thinking or Type of Assessment**	**Vocabulary**	**Scaffolds or Supports**
Learning Progression:				

Source for standard: NGA & CCSSO, 2010b.

Figure 4.3: Example of unpacking process step 2.

In figure 4.3, we circle the words *use, solve,* and *reasoning.* What will the students *use*? They will *use* ratio and rate reasoning, so this is circled. The next circled verb is *solve*; students will *solve* real-world and mathematical problems, so this concept is circled as well. In addition, *reasoning* is circled to indicate students will be able to *reason* about tables of equivalent ratios, tape diagrams, double number line diagrams, or equations.

Step 3: Identify Learning Targets

Teams will write each verb and concept combination in the unpacking chart one at a time (figure 4.4, page 50).

Insert the first verb into the unpacking chart in the column labeled What Will Students Do. Add the knowledge or concepts into the next column, labeled With What Knowledge or Concept. The first verb and concept combination is "use ratio and rate reasoning (to solve real-world and mathematical problems)." The second verb and concept combination is "solve real-world and mathematical problems (using ratio and rate reasoning)," and the third verb and concept combination is "reason about tables of equivalent ratios, tape diagrams, double number line diagrams, or equations." The parentheses around "to solve real-world and mathematical problems" in the first learning target help remind the team that while these skills are unpacked separately, there is a relationship between them that should be honored during instruction. The same is true whenever parentheses appear in the With What Knowledge or Concept column. Unpacking the standard in this way reveals there are three specific learning targets in this standard.

Standard: 6.RP.A.3—(Use) ratio and rate reasoning to (solve) real-world and mathematical problems, such as by (reasoning) about tables of equivalent ratios, tape diagrams, double number line diagrams, or equations.

What Will Students Do (Skills or Verbs)	With What Knowledge or Concept	Level of Thinking or Type of Assessment	Vocabulary	Scaffolds or Supports
Use	Ratio and rate reasoning (to solve real-world and mathematical problems)			
Solve	Real-world and mathematical problems (using ratio and rate reasoning)			
Reason	About tables of equivalent ratios, tape diagrams, double number line diagrams, or equations			
Learning Progression:				

Source for standard: NGA & CCSSO, 2010b.

Figure 4.4: Example of unpacking process step 3.

1. Use ratio and rate reasoning (to solve real-world and mathematical problems).

2. Solve real-world and mathematical problems (using ratio and rate reasoning).

3. Reason about tables of equivalent ratios, tape diagrams, double number line diagrams, or equations.

However, there is no right or wrong way to determine the learning targets in a standard. One team `might unpack this standard keeping it to two targets instead of three. It could decide that the two learning targets are as follows.

1. Use ratio and rate reasoning to solve real-world and mathematical problems.

2. Reason about tables of equivalent ratios, tape diagrams, double number line diagrams, or equations.

It is hard to say which decision is better; there are advantages and disadvantages to both. The biggest advantage to unpacking the standard into three learning targets is that it gives the teacher a delineated list of skills required for mastery of the standard.

If each learning target is assessed as a way of gaining understanding of student progress on the way to mastery of the standard, the teacher will get better information back regarding what skill or concept students could be struggling with. The disadvantage is that these skills and concepts are supposed to be taught and assessed in an integrated way. There is always the risk that learning targets will be taught in isolation of other learning targets that make up the standard when unpacked in this way. This could lead to fractured understanding of concepts and skills for students. Unpacking the standard into two learning targets rather than into three thus gains a distinct advantage in this regard, since the less delineated format makes it more likely that the concepts and skills will be taught and assessed in a more integrated, cohesive manner. The biggest disadvantage to unpacking into two learning targets is less delineated information regarding student progress toward the standard. Through a special education lens, we recommend unpacking into more targets whenever it is logical and possible to do so. More specific information will allow for a more precise understanding of where students may be struggling so that the teacher can provide higher levels of support.

Step 4: Determine the Level of Rigor and Examine Assessment Types

Teams will examine each learning target's complexity and the type of assessment that matches that level of rigor (figure 4.5, page 52).

Any thinking taxonomy can be used to complete this step. We used Webb's Depth of Knowledge (DOK) to identify the level of rigor in our examples (Webb, 2002). In order to determine the rigor of the learning target, you can begin with the verb, but it is important to consider the full context of the standard, as the verb does not always give the complete picture of rigor.

DOK is a scale of cognitive demand (Webb, 2002). It differs from other taxonomies by looking beyond the verb used in the learning target and examining the context in which skills are to be performed and the depth of thinking required. Using the scale can be powerful when teaching students with special needs and may assist, when appropriate, in supporting continued exposure to grade-appropriate standards. The DOK scale has four levels.

1. **Recall:** Level 1 requires rote recall of information, facts, definitions, terms, or simple procedures. The student either knows the answer or does not.

2. **Skills and concepts:** Level 2 requires engagement of mental processing or decision making beyond recall or reproduction. Items falling into this category often have more than one step, such as organizing and comparing data.

Standard: 6.RP.A.3—Use ratio and rate reasoning to solve real-world and mathematical problems, such as by reasoning about tables of equivalent ratios, tape diagrams, double number line diagrams, or equations.				
What Will Students Do (Skills or Verbs)	**With What Knowledge or Concept**	**Level of Thinking or Type of Assessment**	**Vocabulary**	**Scaffolds or Supports**
Use	Ratio and rate reasoning (to solve real-world and mathematical problems)	DOK 2: Multiple choice, constructed response, or performance assessment		
Solve	Real-world and mathematical problems (using ratio and rate reasoning)	DOK 3: Constructed response or performance task		
Reason	About tables of equivalent ratios, tape diagrams, double number line diagrams, or equations	DOK 2: Constructed written response		
Learning Progression:				

Source for standard: NGA & CCSSO, 2010b.

Figure 4.5: Example of unpacking process step 4.

3. **Strategic thinking:** Level 3 requires higher-level thinking than levels 1 and 2 and could include activities or contexts that have more than one possible solution, thereby requiring justification or support for the argument or process.

4. **Extended thinking:** Level 4 requires high-cognitive demand in which students are synthesizing ideas across content areas or situations and generalizing that information to solve new problems. Many responses falling into this category will require extensive time, as they imply that students will be completing multiple steps, such as in a multivariant investigation and analysis.

Let's take a look at the DOK levels and assessment types assigned to the first learning target in our example. In the Level of Thinking or Type of Assessment column, the first learning target, "Use ratio and rate reasoning (to solve real-world and mathematical problems)," was assigned a DOK level 2, as it requires students to use what they know about ratio and rate in order to solve problems, taking the learning target beyond simple recall or reproduction of knowledge. Knowing that the learning target is a DOK level 2 and that we expect more than simple recall, the team should discuss the type of assessment that will best indicate whether students are meeting this expectation at the intended level of rigor. If students are expected to apply their knowledge of ratio and rate in order to solve real-world problems, the assessment questions need to also go beyond simple recall of terms. Notice the types of assessments listed in the example are multiple choice, constructed response, and performance assessment.

A multiple-choice question can be used in this case but should include a scenario where students will need to *use* their understanding of ratio and rate. It would not be appropriate to ask students to identify the definition of rate or ratio when attempting to assess overall student knowledge of this learning target in a summative way. It would be fitting to assess student understanding of the terms as a formative assessment to understand where students are in their knowledge of the basic vocabulary. A constructed-response or performance task makes the most sense for this learning target, as it requires students to construct their own response, not choose an answer from a list, demonstrating their knowledge in a more complete way. This step helps the team scrutinize the intended rigor of each learning target to ensure that there is a strong match between the intended rigor and the level of rigor that students experience during instruction and assessment. More information on assessment is included in chapter 6.

When considering the intended rigor of learning targets, special educators must be careful not to change a target's intended rigor for a student with special needs. It is more effective to determine how instructional scaffolds and supports will be necessary to ensure that students with special needs can meet the intended rigor as opposed to beginning instruction at a grade level lower than the student's age-appropriate placement. This decision demonstrates the commitment to supporting students in truly closing the gap because we continue to focus on their progress toward grade-appropriate learning targets. The decision to modify the rigor of the standards should be limited to our neediest students. Please refer to chapter 3 of this text for guidance in making this determination.

Step 5: Identify Key Vocabulary

Figure 4.6 (page 54) shows how teams will identify the vocabulary that will be explicitly taught to students in order to enhance their understanding of the learning target's components.

Standard: 6.RP.A.3—Use ratio and rate reasoning to solve real-world and mathematical problems, such as by reasoning about tables of equivalent ratios, tape diagrams, double number line diagrams, or equations.

What Will Students Do (Skills or Verbs)	With What Knowledge or Concept	Level of Thinking or Type of Assessment	Vocabulary	Scaffolds or Supports
Use	Ratio and rate reasoning (to solve real-world and mathematical problems)	DOK 2: Multiple choice, constructed response or performance assessment	• Ratio • Rate	
Solve	Real-world and mathematical problems (using ratio and rate reasoning)	DOK 3: Constructed response or performance task	• Solve	
Reason	About tables of equivalent ratios, tape diagrams, double number line diagrams, or equations	DOK 2: Constructed written response	• Equivalent • Diagram • Reason	

Learning Progression:

Source for standard: NGA & CCSSO, 2010b.

Figure 4.6: Example of unpacking process step 5.

We know the importance of vocabulary in learning and the key role it plays in knowledge acquisition across all content areas. According to Marzano (2004), it is essential that subject-specific vocabulary be taught explicitly to students. We have discovered that when teachers highlight the importance of vocabulary embedded in the learning targets, students struggle less with understanding the concepts and skills. For example, when teachers in a district we worked with began to teach vocabulary embedded in the Common Core ELA standards, students could demonstrate understanding of words like *inference*, *theme*, and *judgment* better than they could before these terms were explicitly taught. The teachers also found that they had to provide less intervention and support related to these concepts. This is especially powerful for students with special needs, as they may struggle with vocabulary and can benefit from explicit instruction to help them make sense of the words they will see and hear quite often during instruction and assessment.

Let's take a look at the Common Core mathematics example to identify the specific vocabulary in the first learning target, "Use ratio and rate reasoning (to solve real-world and mathematical problems)." The words *ratio* and *rate* are critical to students' understanding of this learning target. In fact, if students do not understand the definition and applications of ratio and rate, it is unlikely they will be able to solve ratio- and rate-related problems. Therefore, it is imperative that teachers integrate explicit instruction on the meaning and applications of these key terms into their teaching of the standard. Notice that in the remaining learning targets in the example, vocabulary words can be derived directly from the targets themselves. Teams should start building a vocabulary list with these words in the unpacking process, but they may add other key terms as they see fit.

Step 6: Determine a Logical Learning Progression

After working through steps 1–5, the expectations in the standards should begin to emerge, and the team should have a deeper understanding of these expectations. In step 6, the team reviews all information gathered so far in the unpacking process to develop a logical sequence or progression of learning (figure 4.7, page 56).

W. James Popham (2007) defines a learning progression as "a carefully sequenced set of building blocks that students must master en route to mastering a more distant curricular aim" (p. 83). The more distant curricular aim in this case is the learning standard. The learning targets, including consideration of the DOK level and vocabulary, serve as part of the set of building blocks that students must master as they work toward full proficiency of the standard. To develop the set of learning progressions, the team begins by looking at the DOK levels assigned to each learning target and organizing them from simpler to more complex concepts and skills. The team then decides if there is anything that is not explicitly stated in the learning targets that should be added to the progression. In the Common Core mathematics example, we begin the progression with the simple skill of defining and applying the key terms. We feel that it is vital for students to understand and be able to apply these terms in order to navigate real-world problems. We add the idea of applying stamina, grit, and perseverance to the learning progression because we know that while it is not stated directly in the standard or any of the learning targets, poor development of these qualities is part of why students struggle with problem solving. This idea is supported by the work of Angela Duckworth, a psychologist from the University of Pennsylvania who studies grit and perseverance extensively. Her research suggests that grit may be as important as intelligence. In one study, she and her colleagues find that smarter students often have less grit than their peers who score lower on an intelligence test. The study suggests that the students with the most grit, not the

Standard: 6.RP.A.3—~~Use~~ ratio and rate reasoning to ~~solve~~ real-world and mathematical problems, such as by ~~reasoning~~ about tables of equivalent ratios, tape diagrams, double number line diagrams, or equations.

What Will Students Do (Skills or Verbs)	With What Knowledge or Concept	Level of Thinking or Type of Assessment	Vocabulary	Scaffolds or Supports
Use	Ratio and rate reasoning (to solve real-world and mathematical problems)	DOK 2: Multiple choice, constructed response or performance assessment	• Ratio • Rate	
Solve	Real-world and mathematical problems (using ratio and rate reasoning)	DOK 3: Constructed response or performance task	• Solve	
Reason	About tables of equivalent ratios, tape diagrams, double number line diagrams, or equations	DOK 2: Constructed written response	• Equivalent • Diagram • Reason	

Learning Progression:

- Define and apply the concepts of ratio and rate.
- Understand tables of equivalent ratios, tape diagrams, double number line diagrams, or equations as applied to ratio and rate.
- Understand and apply the concept of reasoning.
- Apply stamina, grit, and perseverance to problem solving.
- Navigate real-world problems, break the problem into smaller steps, and apply knowledge.

Source for standard: NGA & CCSSO, 2010b.

Figure 4.7: Example of unpacking process step 6.

smartest ones, actually have the highest GPAs (Duckworth, Peterson, Matthews, & Kelly, 2007). A related study shows students and educators that deliberate practice is not easy and that there will be times when students will struggle, feel confused or frustrated, or be unsure of how to proceed in tasks that require grit and perseverance to complete (Perkins-Gough, 2013). The study theorizes that students' grit levels can be changed by changing their beliefs about trying harder or sticking with it until it is mastered (Perkins-Gough, 2013). What a great message for all educators, especially special educators who work with students who will likely find at least some of the grade-level expectations difficult to master.

The learning progression will assist all educators in determining the best path toward mastery for each student and ensure that before getting to the more difficult concepts, students experience success with some of the simpler concepts. We hope that this success will be beneficial and aid students' stamina, grit, and perseverance when the concepts become more difficult. According to Popham (2007), the learning progression provides a road map that "designates pivotal stops along the way" (p. 83). If the teacher determines the stopping points before instruction begins, it is far easier to incorporate them during instruction and assessment. The progression provides teachers with a systematic way to "collect evidence of a student's progress toward mastery" of the standard (Popham, 2007, p. 83). Here's the good news: Popham (2007) contends that "there is no single, universally accepted and absolutely correct learning progression underlying any given high-level curricular aim" (p. 84). "Thoughtful, well-intentioned educators" can end with strikingly different learning progressions, but the key is that "almost any carefully conceived learning progression is more likely to benefit students than teachers' off-the-cuff decision making" (Popham, 2007, p. 84). Examining the learning progression leads to the next step in the process: determining potential scaffolds and supports students may need along the way.

Step 7: Determine Potential Scaffolds and Supports

It is inevitable that some students will struggle with the targets the learning progressions outline. Determining potential scaffolds and supports as figure 4.8 (page 58) illustrates is a critically important step to ensure that all students learn.

In this step, educators consider the scaffolds and supports that students may need before instruction begins; adding to and adapting this list after examining student work or assessments gives teachers even more information about where students specifically struggle. Our ideas for scaffolds and supports around the first learning target, "Use ratio and rate reasoning (to solve real-world and mathematical problems)," include vocabulary practice for students who are having difficulty understanding the concepts. We suggest simpler problems to build skills, eventually moving to more complex problems. Yet when choosing to use simpler versions, always keep in mind that the goal is for all students to master the grade-level expectations, so it is critical to continue raising the bar as educators provide scaffolds and supports. Throughout the example, we have used scaffolds and supports that have worked for us and for the teachers with whom we have worked. There are numerous approaches to providing support, and part of the value of teams working together on this process is to learn the different strategies that have been successful for various team members.

Standard: 6.RP.A.3—Use ratio and rate reasoning to solve real-world and mathematical problems, such as by reasoning about tables of equivalent ratios, tape diagrams, double number line diagrams, or equations.

What Will Students Do (Skills or Verbs)	With What Knowledge or Concept	Level of Thinking or Type of Assessment	Vocabulary	Scaffolds or Supports
Use	Ratio and rate reasoning (to solve real-world and mathematical problems)	DOK 2: Multiple choice, constructed response or performance assessment	• Ratio • Rate	• Use vocabulary practice or small-group work. • Practice mathematical problems with simpler numbers or variables. Once a student demonstrates mastery on these, add problems with more complex numbers or variables. • Use video clips to demonstrate a process, skill, or concept with student access available for repeated viewings. • Show and brainstorm the different ways that ratios are written—2 to 5, 2/5, 2:5, 40%, 0.4 are all different ways of describing the same ratio.
Solve	Real-world and mathematical problems (using ratio and rate reasoning)	DOK 3: Constructed response or performance task	• Solve	• Model problem-solving strategies, or practice in small groups. • Help students visualize the problem, or act out the problem using manipulatives.
Reason	About tables of equivalent ratios, tape diagrams, double number line diagrams, or equations	DOK 2: Constructed written response	• Equivalent • Diagram • Reason	• Practice reasoning with less complex tables, and so on.

Learning Progression:

• Define and apply the concepts of ratio and rate.

• Understand tables of equivalent ratios, tape diagrams, double number line diagrams, or equations as applied to ratio and rate.

• Understand and apply the concept of reasoning.

• Apply stamina, grit, and perseverance to problem solving.

• Navigate real-world problems, break down the problem into smaller steps, and apply knowledge.

Source for standard: NGA & CCSSO, 2010b.

Figure 4.8: Example of unpacking process step 7.

Various researchers and experts in specific content areas provide research-based strategies that may help teams when completing this part of the unpacking process. For example, Russell Gersten, Lynn S. Fuchs, Joanna P. Williams, and Scott Baker (2001) review effective instructional methods for reading comprehension with narrative and expository text for students with special needs. Erica R. Kaldenberg, Sarah J. Watt, and William J. Therrien (2015) examine reading instruction in science for students with learning disabilities and provide effective ways to increase reading comprehension of expository science texts. The University of Kansas Center for Research on Learning provides myriad strategies for areas such as reading, writing, mathematics, motivation, information recall, and interpersonal interaction, all focused on helping students understand information and solve problems effectively. Visit the center's website at www.kucrl.org/sim/strategies.shtml for more information. We worked with special educators who used the center's sentence-writing and paragraph-writing strategies with great success. The teachers report marked improvement in their students' district writing benchmark assessments and are inspired by their students' abilities to apply the strategies in writing across content areas.

Figure 4.9 (pages 60–61) illustrates the entire unpacking process with two Common Core Reading standards unpacked in the same form to honor the importance of integrating two standards for instruction and assessment purposes.

Engagement in the processes this chapter outlines will move individuals and teams closer to a guaranteed and viable curriculum that provides a more consistent picture of what *all* students are expected to learn as well as what mastery of the standards looks like. All educators, but specifically those who work with students with special needs, will benefit from this consistent, commonly understood, and complete picture of student learning. Jason Keenon, an informational literacy coach in Kildeer Countryside Community Consolidated School District 96, participated in this process with his general education colleagues for units of instruction aligned to the College, Career, and Civic Life (C3) Framework for Social Studies State Standards (National Council for the Social Studies, 2010). He expressed appreciation for the opportunity to walk away with an instructional plan that had already considered the supports and scaffolds his students might need as they work toward mastery of the standards (J. Keenon, personal communication, January 22, 2016). The collaborative discussions on teaching and learning provided him an opportunity not only to gain clarity regarding the standards' expectations but also to assist general educators in truly understanding the type of instruction students with special needs must have in order to learn successfully. Most important, he described the value of this work for his students as priceless, articulating the significant difference he can make for them when he considers each aspect of instruction carefully and thoughtfully for a unit of instruction with a focus on individual student needs. This process allows teachers to

Standards: RL.6.1—Cite textual evidence to support analysis of what the text says explicitly as well as inferences drawn from the text.

RL.6.2—Determine a theme or central idea of a text and how it is conveyed through particular details; provide a summary of the text distinct from personal opinions or judgments.

What Will Students Do (Skills or Verbs)	With What Knowledge or Concept	Level of Thinking or Type of Assessment	Vocabulary	Scaffolds or Supports
Cite	Textual evidence to support analysis of text	DOK 2: Constructed response	• Cite • Evidence • Analysis	Read the text and determine where students might struggle with text complexity.
Analyze	What the text says explicitly using textual evidence	DOK 2: A/B multiple choice (evidence-based selected response) or constructed response	• Explicitly	• Model analysis using evidence. • See the last three rows of this chart to embed analysis of evidence with theme.
Analyze	Inferences drawn from the text using textual evidence	DOK 3: A/B multiple choice (evidence-based selected response) and constructed response	• Inference	• Ensure understanding of inference. • See the last three rows of this chart to embed analysis of evidence with theme.
Determine	A theme or central idea of a text	DOK 1: Multiple choice or short answer	• Determine • Theme or central idea	• Use vocabulary. • Build background knowledge. • Build skill by practicing identifying theme from short passages or small groups. • Guide annotation with sticky notes in small groups. • Use close reading with focus on questions leading to theme identification.

Determine	How theme is conveyed through particular details	DOK 2: Multiple choice or constructed response	• Conveyed • Details	• Guide practice identifying details in small groups. • Use card sorting with details on each card, or sort cards aligned to theme. • Use close reading with focus on questions leading to identification of important details.
Provide	A summary of the text distinct from personal opinions or judgments	DOK 2: Performance task	• Summary • Distinct • Opinion • Judgment	• Use guided practice in summary writing steps. • Use a graphic organizer to pull theme or details together to guide writing of the summary.

Learning Progression:

- Understand the key vocabulary as used in the standards (**cite, evidence, analysis, explicitly, inference, determine, theme or central idea, conveyed, details, summary, distinct, opinion, judgment**).
- Understand how details in a text (evidence) help convey theme.
- Identify how theme is conveyed through particular details in a text, and be able to cite these details as textual evidence.
- Understand the components of a quality summary.
- Understand how to write a summary based on details (evidence) from the text opposed to opinions and judgments.
- Write a summary that describes the theme of a story with supporting details (evidence) from the text.

Source for standards: NGA & CCSSO, 2010a.

Figure 4.9: Unpacking two interrelated Common Core ELA standards.

Visit go.solution-tree.com/PLCbooks for a free reproducible version of this figure.

provide consistent, rigorous instruction for *all* students so that they can be successful when they enter college or the workforce.

Yes We Can: Keys to Moving Forward

By determining what teachers expect students to know and be able to do, prioritizing the list of expectations and standards, and unpacking the priority standards, collaborative teams take action to support students and provide a clear path to mastery. As you work in collaborative teams on these action steps, remember the following keys to moving forward.

- Define and develop a shared understanding of what students should know and be able to do before beginning a unit of instruction.

- Prioritize the standards collaboratively, or else individual teachers will prioritize anyway, leading to differences in what students in the same grade or course learn.

- Take the time to unpack the standards collaboratively because the knowledge teachers gain from the process will benefit students.

- Use learning progressions to plan instruction and assessment and to guide interventions.

Now that teams have a solid understanding of the unpacking process, chapter 5 prepares them to design standards-aligned instruction for all learners.

CHAPTER 5

DESIGNING STANDARDS-ALIGNED INSTRUCTION FOR STUDENT SUCCESS

Treat people as if they were what they ought to be and you help them become what they are capable of being.

—Johann Wolfgang von Goethe

Educators across the United States are designing lesson plans that meet the expectations and higher level of academic rigor that the CCSS require. For those U.S. states that have not adopted the CCSS, the expectations either continue to be high or have increased. No matter what standards guide teaching and learning in your state, the instructional shifts outline what we are all striving for as we work to prepare students for their futures.

The increase in and expectations of rigor provide a challenge and an opportunity. The challenge is that many students will need significant support and scaffolding in order to meet the more rigorous expectations. We also have the great opportunity to develop students who have the knowledge, skills, and mindsets to be successful in anything they choose to do. How do we rise to this challenge and opportunity for students with special needs and others who will need high levels of support and guidance in order to meet these expectations? This chapter focuses on how to plan for specially designed instruction tailored to meet these students' needs.

Defining Instructional Shifts

The CCSS and other revised standards have brought to the forefront the importance of preparing students for what they will be expected to know and be able to do in college and careers. Standards help define the instructional shifts necessary to ensure that students are prepared for the world ahead. Tables 5.1 and 5.2 summarize the CCSS instructional shifts in English language arts and mathematics, respectively, and address the implications the shifts have for teaching students with special needs.

Table 5.1: CCSS English Language Arts Instructional Shifts

Shifts	Implications for Teaching Students With Special Needs
Balancing informational and literary text: Students read a true balance of informational and literary texts.	Teachers expose all students to complex informational texts, instead of avoiding it out of frustration.
Knowledge in the disciplines: Students build knowledge about the world (domains and content areas) through text rather than from the teacher or activities.	Teachers provide opportunities for students to read the text and support them through careful scaffolding to increase comprehension. The teacher keeps the focus on the text, not on teacher-created PowerPoint presentations and notes that provide information from the text to students so they do not have to struggle with difficult text.
Staircase of complexity: Teachers are patient and create more time, space, and support in the curriculum for close reading of complex text at the appropriate text complexity for the grade level. The staircase of complexity implies that there are ranges of text complexity appropriate for each grade level and that teachers should use text that is within the range during instruction.	Teachers provide complex text as well as the scaffolds and strategies necessary for students to learn how to navigate it. They focus the majority of instruction on grade-level-appropriate text. Occasionally moving to a lower level of complexity may be necessary for some students to assist their ability to comprehend the more difficult grade-level text. It is imperative that teachers give all students opportunities to experience rigorous grade-level text.
Text-based answers: Students engage in rich and rigorous evidence-based conversations about text.	Teachers provide opportunities for students to discuss text using complex questions. They avoid lowering the rigor of the question or task and instead guide students through the complex questions and tasks.
Writing from sources: Students' writing emphasizes use of evidence from sources to inform or make an argument.	Teachers give students opportunities to write often, and they provide lots of growth-producing feedback.
Academic vocabulary: Students constantly build the transferable vocabulary they need to access grade-level complex texts. This can be done effectively by spiraling like content in increasingly complex texts.	Teachers always keep vocabulary at the forefront of teaching and learning; they return to vocabulary when students need support for learning.

Source: Adapted from Engage New York, 2012.

Table 5.2: CCSS Mathematics Instructional Shifts

Shifts	Implications for Teaching Students With Special Needs
Focus: Teachers significantly narrow and deepen the scope of how time and energy are spent in the mathematics classroom to focus only on the concepts they prioritized from the standards.	Teachers focus on the priority concepts and skills to narrow support areas.
Coherence: Principals and teachers carefully connect learning within and across grades so that students can build new understanding onto foundations built in previous years.	Teachers make connections clear and explicit using real-life examples. Teachers use common language.
Fluency: Students develop speed and accuracy with simple calculations. Teachers structure class time, homework time, or both for students to memorize core functions through repetition.	Teachers foster fluency through repetition, using visuals and manipulatives.
Deep understanding: Students deeply understand and can operate easily within a mathematics concept before moving on. They learn more than the trick to get the answer right; they learn the mathematics.	Teachers give students practice with simpler concepts and work up to more complex skills. Teachers use manipulatives to demonstrate concepts.
Application: Students are expected to use mathematics and choose the appropriate concept for application even when they are not prompted to do so.	Teachers give students opportunities to practice application of concepts in simple to more complex scenarios.
Dual intensity: Students are practicing and understanding. There is more than a balance between these two things in the classroom—both are occurring with intensity.	Teachers use visual models and manipulatives to deepen students' understanding as they practice concepts and skills.

Source: Adapted from Engage New York, 2012.

In addition to the previously mentioned shifts, students who meet the expectations of the CCSS will ideally demonstrate independence; have strong content knowledge; be able to respond to varying demands of audience, task, purpose, and discipline; comprehend as well as critique; value evidence; use technology and digital media strategically and capably; and understand other perspectives and cultures (NGA & CCSSO, 2010a). Isn't this what we want for all students? Educators often agree that this is what they want for their students, but they are unsure how to accomplish these aims when they have to consider mastery of learning targets, skill-deficit remediation, and a myriad of other considerations for students with special needs. This is not a simple answer, but we can certainly start with structures for focusing on the expectations in the standards and then determining the most responsive scaffolds and supports, tailoring instruction accordingly.

Tailoring Instruction for Students With Special Needs

Tailoring instruction in English language arts and mathematics for students with special needs is often the most challenging instructional demand for educators to navigate. Educators want their students to feel successful, so they sometimes make decisions that are actually detrimental to students, like lowering text-complexity expectations or overly modifying an assignment, task, or assessment to the point that the intended rigor is virtually nonexistent.

The majority of students with special needs are capable of much more than that. One analysis of fourth-grade mathematics scores shows that like their general education peers, some students with special needs scored low on the assessment, and others scored high. Several students with special needs were capable enough to score at the high end of proficiency with their general education peers (Gong & Simpson, 2005). These data are just one example of why it is imperative that we do not assume that *special needs* means *incapable*.

According to Michael Yudin (2014), acting assistant secretary for the Office of Special Education and Rehabilitative Services at the U.S. Department of Education, many of the students with special needs in the United States leave high school without the knowledge and skills necessary to be successful in the world. In fact, he contends that "fewer than 10 percent of eighth graders with special needs score proficient in reading and mathematics on the National Assessment of Educational Progress (NAEP)" (Yudin, 2014). He claims that this is partly due to the fact that educational opportunities for students with special needs are limited by low expectations for these students. Yudin (2014) urges us to "do better" and "have higher expectations for our [students], and to hold ourselves accountable as a nation for their success."

To further illustrate this point, let's consider PLC question 4: How will we respond when some students already know it? Undoubtedly, there will be students with special needs who will demonstrate deep understanding of some concepts and skills before instruction occurs or very early in a unit of instruction. Collaborative teams of general and special educators need to consider the factors that led to the student's success when he or she demonstrates high levels of proficiency with particular learning targets or curricular concepts and use that information to guide instruction in other curriculum areas. It is an opportunity to see the special education student through his or her strengths, not just the student's deficits. According to authors Donald O. Clifton and James K. Harter (2003), "Individuals gain more when they build on their talents than when they make comparable efforts to improve their areas of weakness" (p. 112). When students spend most of their time in their area of weakness, as most students with special needs do, their skills will likely improve, but this common approach does not always lead to student motivation or high levels of student engagement.

The greatest challenge we face as educators is how to engage the hearts and minds of our students. Focusing on their strengths gives us the opportunity to start seeing special education students in terms of who they are rather than who they are not (Clifton & Anderson, 2002). In his book, *Neurodiversity in the Classroom: Strength-Based Strategies to Help Students With Special Needs Succeed in School and Life*, Thomas Armstrong (2012) helps us put this in perspective when he asks readers to think about their greatest academic or nonacademic difficulty or limitation in life. He asks them to imagine that:

> [They] have been tested and found in need of support in this area, and that they will then be sent to a special program where they spend most of their time focusing on that area. It does not sound like the best scenario for success, yet this is what many students in special education face on a daily basis. (p. 2)

Instead, he suggests focusing on student strengths as the starting point when helping students with special needs achieve success in school and life. Think about students with special needs as assets instead of liabilities. As Armstrong (2012) notes:

> If our only knowledge about students with special needs is limited to the negatives in their lives—low test scores, low grades, negative behavior reports, and deficit-oriented diagnostic labels—then our ability to differentiate learning effectively is significantly restricted. (p. 13)

While it is critically important to meet the identified needs of special education students, it is also important to emphasize what students know and can do well. This balance gives us the opportunity to celebrate and build on our students' strengths.

We can begin to ensure that students with special needs receive the type of instruction that will honor their abilities and strengths and ensure that they are exposed to high-quality rigorous instruction by tailoring instruction for students in a way that gives them the best chance for success. To effectively tailor instruction, educators must agree that tailored instruction for students with special needs does *not* mean:

- Lowering the expectation of the standard or teaching to lower grade-level standards

- Eliminating the more complex components of a standard, task, text, or concept

- Consistently using materials or resources that are not at grade-level expectations

- Providing texts that are lower in complexity than those in the grade-level text-complexity band

- Rescuing students when a task or concept is difficult for them

If we agree that the points describe what tailored instruction does *not* mean, what *does* it mean? Table 5.3 outlines our definitions.

Table 5.3: Tailored Instruction for Students With Special Needs

Tailored Instruction Does Not Mean	Tailored Instruction Means
Lowering the expectation of the standard or teaching to lower grade-level standards	Unpacking the grade-level standard (see chapter 4), determining a logical learning progression task, and anticipating where students might need support and scaffolds to successfully master the standard
Eliminating the more complex components of a standard, task, text, or concept	Unpacking the grade-level standard (see chapter 4), identifying the most rigorous components of the standard, and analyzing the learning progression to determine how to ensure students master the most rigorous standard components
Consistently using materials or resources that are not at grade-level expectations	Beginning with grade-level materials and resources and analyzing the learning progression to anticipate prior to instruction how each resource will need to be scaffolded for each student
Providing texts that are lower in complexity than those in the grade-level text-complexity band	Beginning with grade-level text and analyzing the learning progression to anticipate prior to instruction how the text and the instruction will need to be scaffolded for students who are not currently reading at grade level
Rescuing students when a task or concept is difficult for them	Allowing students to engage in productive struggle, anticipating where this might happen and planning for it, and watching for signs of destructive struggle

Let's look at these criteria to gain a deeper understanding of five actions teachers must take to ensure they will effectively tailor instruction: (1) unpacking standards and examining logical learning progressions, (2) attending to the most complex aspects of the standards, (3) focusing on materials and resources used for instruction, (4) scaffolding instruction and text to support reading at grade level, and (5) planning for and allowing productive struggle, while watching for destructive struggle.

Unpacking Standards and Examining Logical Learning Progressions

Tailored instruction requires that educators unpack standards to identify what students are expected to know and be able to do in order to anticipate student needs and plan for appropriate supports and scaffolds. The unpacking process provides an opportunity for deep understanding of the student expectations embedded in the standards and allows teachers to thoughtfully consider the best approaches to instruction based on student needs. Recognizing that a diverse classroom is the norm rather than the exception, special and general educators must anticipate that in order for all students to learn the expected standards, they must provide responsive instruction that considers not only attaining proficiency in the standards, but also the students' individual differences, including culture, interests, and prior experiences. Teachers can use this information to provide meaningful learning experiences for each student.

Careful consideration of the learning progression toward mastery is essential, as teachers can anticipate where students may struggle based on knowledge of each student's instructional needs and design instruction accordingly. This topic is explored in detail in chapter 4.

Attending to the Most Complex Aspects of the Standards

Unpacking standards increases teachers' knowledge of the most demanding components of the standards. Understanding the learning progression and the complexity of the skills a standard requires helps teachers plan time and support appropriately to ensure students master these components. The lower-complexity learning targets of the learning progression should take less time and require less support and scaffolding than the more complex components of the learning progression, so teachers should plan to spend more time on the more complex components of instruction. If a student continues to struggle with the less complex knowledge and skills, consider adding more time and individualized support (such as before or after school, at lunch, and so on) for the student to ensure that he or she has the opportunity to learn the more complex aspects of the standard.

Focusing on Materials and Resources Used for Instruction

We believe that the majority of materials and resources used for instruction should be at grade level or above and that it is not acceptable practice to teach sixth graders with third- or fourth-grade-level textbooks and materials. While it may be acceptable to use some off-grade-level materials occasionally as part of the scaffolding process, it is essential that students experience and learn to navigate grade-level material.

Scaffolding Instruction and Text to Support Reading at Grade Level

Scaffolding text is critical to ensure educators meet the needs of struggling readers. It is also a controversial topic among literacy experts. For many years, literacy experts have contended that students should be taught at their instructional level, which is determined through a combination of word recognition and ability to answer questions about the text. Theoretically, a book at students' instructional level is one that:

> allows them to gain accuracy, fluency, and comprehension, while providing some problem solving challenges along the way. By reading these leveled books, students extend their knowledge and skill of reading by engaging with texts that have the right mixture of support and challenge for the reader. (Strauss, 2014)

This means that a fifth-grade student could have an instructional level equivalent to a third-grade level of text complexity and would be instructed using text at the third-grade level. While there have always been some who have rejected this notion, most were content to continue this practice, as it was what the experts said was the right thing to do. In fact, it is still widely accepted as appropriate for students in kindergarten through second grade. According to Timothy Shanahan (2014a), a distinguished professor emeritus of urban education at the University of Illinois at Chicago, the Common Core has been the driver of this debate about text complexity:

> The controversy has been brought about by Common Core, since those standards are specific about the difficulty level of the texts that students need to learn to read. Unlike past standards that ignored what students could read, CCSS specifies particular levels of text difficulty for each grade two through twelve. They did this basically because if students were taught at their instructional levels all the time, how would they ever reach college or career readiness by the time they leave high school.

Shanahan (2011) believes that "challenging text is the right ground to maximize student learning" and that "students need the greatest scaffolding and support from the teacher when reading the hardest texts" (Shanahan, 2014b). Shanahan believes that the teacher, not the text, is the scaffold. We fully recognize that teachers need sustained, focused professional development in order to learn the best strategies for scaffolding complex text for struggling readers. For this shift to gain traction in schools across the United States, the key will be a change in mindset regarding what students are capable of as well as in teacher understanding of how to "be the scaffold" for students as they work through more complex texts.

So what is an educator to do? We believe that the best thing to do is give students opportunities to experience text at their instructional level and at grade level. When using grade-level text that is difficult for students, provide support and scaffolds for students so that they learn how to navigate challenging texts. By supplying heavy doses of teacher support and scaffolds, and then gradually releasing them, educators help students develop a toolbox of strategies to use whenever they encounter complex texts, which they often will in their academic careers as well as in the workforce.

Planning for and Allowing Productive Struggle

Let's take a deeper look into what productive struggle means, what it looks like, what happens when struggle is productive, and how to determine when it becomes destructive.

It is difficult for teachers to watch students struggle, just like it is difficult for parents to watch their children struggle, but what we need to remember is that struggle can be a good thing. In fact, the famous words of abolitionist Frederick Douglass's 1857 West India emancipation speech still resonate: "If there is no struggle, there is no progress" (Douglass, 1985, p. 204). How can we provide experiences for students that allow just the right amount of struggle so that they make progress, and how does consideration of this balance impact how we define what it means to advocate for students with special needs? In an interview with Rick Allen (2012), author Robyn Jackson points out that destructive struggle happens when students run out of strategies and essentially give up. This is where a teacher might see a frustrated, deflated, or even angry student. Jackson and Lambert (2010) caution that these reactions can be a result of learned helplessness. The student may have relied on the teacher's help so much so that he or she is not sure what to do when the teacher is not there (Allen, 2012). When we continue to rescue students who struggle, we are in danger of creating this type of scenario, the very one that teachers are trying desperately to avoid. Because they care about the social and emotional well-being of their students, teachers do not want students to be frustrated or angry, so they swoop in and rescue them. Unfortunately, this can backfire and actually cause the student more frustration when the student is working at home or any time the teacher is unavailable.

We believe a key to avoiding destructive struggle and promoting productive struggle is a thorough, thoughtful planning process before instruction begins. The unpacking process and careful development of learning progressions will help educators think through instruction, determining what each student may need to be successful. This process will help educators consider a plan for how and when they will intervene with students who still need some support, while at the same time working to develop the learning of students who have the grit and stamina to persevere through challenging tasks. In her conversation with Rick Allen (2012), Robyn Jackson suggests that we do not need to look for "big symptoms with big solutions." Instead, we can provide feedback, suggest strategies and tools to try, or provide a peer tutor. Robyn Jackson reminds us that "One of the key signs of rigor is independent thinking and learning" (as cited in Allen, 2012). If we want our students to be prepared for college and careers, we should be fostering independence as much as we are academic content. This is part of rigorous teaching and learning. Jackson points out that "rigor requires rigor—if we want to develop rigorous learning and thinking for our kids, then we have to be more rigorous in our teaching" (as cited in Allen, 2012). To help foster independence, it is important to allow students to struggle, but educators must discern between productive and destructive struggle and intervene appropriately. Table 5.4 contrasts the characteristics of productive and destructive struggle.

Table 5.4: Productive Versus Destructive Struggle

Productive Struggle	Destructive Struggle
Leads to understanding	Leads to frustration
Makes learning goals feel attainable and worthwhile	Makes learning goals feel hazy and out of reach
Yields results	Feels fruitless
Leads students to feelings of empowerment and efficacy	Leaves students feeling abandoned and on their own
Creates a sense of hope	Creates a sense of inadequacy

Source: Jackson & Lambert, 2010, p. 54.

Without question, meeting the needs of *all* students is a complex process that requires teachers to think carefully and deeply about each student's identified areas of deficit and strengths in order to provide instruction that moves the student closer to mastering or even extending grade-level expectations and IEP goals. We hope that the ideas and processes outlined in this chapter will provide teachers and teams the opportunity to provide rigorous, responsive instruction for all students.

Yes We Can: Keys to Moving Forward

As you work with your team on the five actions outlined in this chapter to tailor instruction effectively for all students, consider the following keys to moving forward.

- Communicate to students often through your actions and words that you believe they are capable of achieving their goals.

- Tailor instruction to provide support, keeping expectations high.

- Identify student strengths and capitalize on them.

- Allow students to struggle productively.

Chapter 6 considers how instruction and assessment work together in a standards-aligned system.

CHAPTER 6

DETERMINING CRITERIA FOR ASSESSMENT

Formative assessment represents evidence-based instructional decision-making. If you want to become more instructionally effective, and if you want your students to achieve more, then formative assessments should be for you.

—W. James Popham

How will we know when students have learned? The answer lies in standards-aligned assessments. When you ask most educators their thoughts about assessment, however, you can almost count on a less-than-positive response. Why is this? Why has *assessment* become a veritable curse word?

Many teachers will claim that they are not assessment experts. That couldn't be further from the truth. In fact, research supports that teacher-created assessments provide the practical utility we need to measure student learning and maximize progress toward the standards we prioritize (Reeves, 2007). When teachers determine the criteria for assessment, they more deeply understand the criteria for success and, therefore, design instruction so students succeed. This is the best possible scenario for all students but specifically for those with special needs. Only a teacher who understands the ending target can create the instructional plan that leads each individual learner to mastery. For students with special needs, this personalized learning plan is essential to proficiency and growth.

Before focusing on a method to align standards or IEP goals to assessments, it is essential to understand there are many types of, and purposes for, assessment. In our experience, educators who have a negative view of assessment do not understand that assessment practices follow a continuum of types and purposes.

We'll use a car's tire condition to describe a commonly used assessment process. What if, for example, a driver notices the car shaking while driving but does nothing about it? Taking no interim steps, the driver is likely to experience a blowout. On the other hand, if the driver notices the shake and responds by immediately purchasing new tires, he or she likely overreacts to the situation and spends money on repairs that perhaps aren't needed. Aligning the situation to the assessment and action steps is crucial to monitoring and responding to the current reality in a way that makes sense given the timing and scope of the event. It ultimately leads to more informed and accurate decision making.

So how does this come to life when we think about education? Let's consider these connections in table 6.1.

Table 6.1: Continuum of Assessment

Most Formative: Classroom Assessments	Formative: Team Common Assessments	Summative: Benchmark Assessments	Most Summative: Accountability Assessments
• Ensure ongoing monitoring of student learning. • Drive day-to-day instruction.	• Ensure consistency in curriculum across a team. • Allow for team discussion of student-performance data and aligned collaborative planning of instruction and assessment.	• Ensure equity, alignment, and pacing of standards. • Determine progress toward achievement on year-end accountability assessments. • Provide data to identify individual students who need additional time and support. • Provide data to determine the effectiveness of curriculum and instruction to make changes for the following year.	• Ensure that systems focus on the agreed-on standards. • Measure student learning per state guidelines to indicate if students have learned, in a grade level or course, what they are expected to have mastered.

Clearly, assessments within the continuum are defined differently and are used for different purposes. Note that there are two common factors that connect all assessments at all levels of the continuum.

1. **They all align to the identified standards** (most often the applicable state or national standards).

2. **They all align to the agreed-on pacing** developed externally or by internal teams.

With these two common criteria in mind, let's consider what the continuum of assessment types looks like in the school environment, starting with the most formative and moving toward the most summative. Table 6.2 provides common classroom scenarios along the continuum of assessments.

Table 6.2: Continuum of Classroom Assessments

Scenario	Aligned Assessment Type
A classroom teacher monitors students as they are working by using checklists, by taking anecdotal notes, or by using teacher-developed "checks" (quizzes, exit slips, and so on).	Most formative assessment
A team of teachers who teach the same content develop common assessments to be given every two weeks of instruction. They use the data from these to plan instruction, identify students who need more time and support, identify students who are ready for additional rigor, and support each other's professional growth.	Formative assessment
At the end of a unit of instruction, all teachers of the same content give the same assessment to report on student learning.	Summative assessment
At the specified time, all teachers of the same content give the same external assessment to report on students' annual progress.	Most summative assessment

When considered in this way, it is easy to see that there is no wrong assessment; rather, there are different types of assessments used for different purposes.

Doing only one type of assessment, however, *is* a problem—particularly when we think about students with special needs. Whether we are teachers, principals, related-services providers, district administrators, or other personnel who support students with special needs, if we wait until the end of the year or the IEP's annual review to check in on student learning, we cannot possibly adjust instruction to address needs as they arise.

Let's examine the experience of one high school teacher. One of the teacher's students struggles to comprehend grade-level text, and the teacher has indicated overcoming this struggle as an IEP goal. If the teacher waits until the final exam, the IEP reporting window, or worse yet, the end of the IEP window, three questions present themselves.

1. **How can the teacher adjust instruction to meet the student's specific needs?** For example, does the student struggle more or differently with literature compared to informational text? Given the answer to this question, the teacher needs to provide different support. In the absence of an answer, the teacher cannot tailor instruction as needed.

2. **Is the student making progress toward the identified goals?** Without a regular check-in, it is impossible to know if the instruction provided is actually making a difference for the student.

3. **Most important, is the student making progress toward grade-level expectations?** Regularly and formatively assessing the student's progress toward grade-level standards is the only way to ensure that the student is truly closing the gap. Conversely, not doing so almost guarantees that the student will never reach grade-level expectations.

Aligning Instruction and Assessment

In chapter 4, we advocate for a process to prioritize standards and a consistent approach to unpacking standards. This process helps teachers develop a shared understanding of the standards' nuances and prioritize them purposefully. This first step must be completed before a teacher, team, school, or system creates assessments.

However, there are some essential points to keep in mind in moving from unpacking to assessment writing. When considering assessment methods, there are two myths we would like to discuss.

1. **Selected-response items are not good indicators of student learning:** There are times that a multiple-choice or fill-in-the-blank item is the appropriate fit. When a standard focuses on verbs requiring recall, a well-written selected-response item can be a valid and efficient way to determine student understanding.

2. **Performance tasks are always the best way to measure student learning:** Projects, portfolios, and performances can be outstanding ways to assess. However, they often require a great deal of time for students to complete and for teachers to analyze in order to determine student mastery.

The bottom line in assessment design is that teacher teams must consider the meaning of the standard and then determine the best measure of assessing it.

Developing the Assessment

Once a collaborative team has unpacked and prioritized standards and determined the level of rigor and types of appropriate assessments, the last piece is to develop the assessment. While there aren't specific rules for this, the process almost always naturally develops when the assessors have collaborated on the action steps outlined in chapter 4. When the standard is clearly understood, the standard's rigor is agreed on, and the appropriate assessment method is determined, the creation of the assessment itself tends to be the easiest part. In our experience, the following three tips can help teams create assessments.

1. **Use resources you already have to create assessment items:** While there is value in teachers writing the items, there is also nothing wrong with using already existing resources, as long as the team considers items with the expected rigor of the task in mind.

2. **Remember that one well-planned constructed-response item or performance task can be enough:** When teacher teams purposefully create a more complex task and develop common scoring criteria, it can become a meaningful artifact that informs us about student learning on one, or even more than one, standard.

3. **Remember that one well-planned selected-response item is *not always* enough:** In order to determine student mastery of a recall-level item, it is absolutely necessary to provide multiple selected-response questions. There is no magic number; rather, the quantity is a conversation for the collaborative team, which will need to determine how many items will help teachers confidently know that students can demonstrate the skill.

These tips are effective and efficient in planning instruction and assessment for all learners, especially for students with special needs. After a team creates well-designed assessments aligned to the grade-level standards, it can develop an instructional plan that helps students build skills and knowledge sequentially to demonstrate proficiency on assessments. As the team plans instruction with the assessments in mind, it can also anticipate where students may struggle and proactively plan for ways to differentiate, scaffold, or even modify instruction so that the unique needs of students with special needs can be met. Proactive planning results in a far greater chance that *all* students will demonstrate mastery on the identified standards in the given unit of instruction. When students need additional support and scaffolding to reach the grade-level standards, this approach is invaluable. When students do not have mastery of the prerequisite skills for a standard, it is easy to see how a teacher can do the following.

- Examine the verb to ensure that the student can work at this level
- Focus on a verb at a lower level of rigor to build the student's prerequisite knowledge and skills and assess the student's mastery at the given skill level
- Return to the verb indicated in the grade-level standard when the student masters the prerequisite skill, providing the scaffolding and support the student needs to be able to work at the lower-level expectation and continue to assess, keeping in mind the verb's level of rigor

When students are significantly discrepant from the grade-level standard, educators must apply these same practices but study even more deeply the skills that the standards require. For example, if a language arts standard requires students to compare the themes of two texts, a critical prerequisite skill is that students must first be able to identify the theme in a single text. If the student cannot demonstrate this skill first, it will be impossible for him or her to find success on the standard requiring him or her to compare themes in two different texts. It would be an incredible disservice to the student for the teaching team to ignore the standard's prerequisite skills and fail to support the student in mastering the prerequisite skill prior to measuring his or her mastery of the more rigorous standard. By skipping these steps, a student may present as though he or she cannot complete the more rigorous task when, in reality, he or she may very likely be able to once he or she has mastered the fundamental skill required. Collaborative teams can help ensure that students receive the support they need to master missing prerequisite skills at or below grade level and can monitor progress toward mastering the more rigorous grade-level standard. By collaborating in this way with a purposeful focus on each standard and its prerequisite skills, educators can offer the support all students need to learn and demonstrate proficiency.

Designing a Specialized Curriculum

What about our students who need a specialized curriculum designed for their skill set based on their unique and current performance level? The team of professionals working with such students follows the same protocols to ensure shared understanding of the standards and expectations, while staying focused on two slightly different questions.

1. What do we expect *this* student to know and be able to do?
2. How will we measure progress for *this* student?

The team then designs assessments to measure student progress along the way. For students in this scenario, the team will likely lean on performance tasks if the student's skill set is best measured by monitoring his or her completion of finite tasks in order to observe the skills that the student can demonstrate in a way that is meaningful and functional for the student. Examples may include sorting of functional objects; completing self-help routines; using eye gaze to express understanding; and using augmentative communication devices (such as switches, iPads, and talk boxes) to express wants, needs, and knowledge.

The commitment to collecting data regularly to measure progress, refine instruction, and provide more or different scaffolding does not change. However, the scope of the work shifts from *all students at the grade level* to *this student with this skill set at this point in time*. Collaborative teams must determine how to collect data in such a way that it is formative and drives instruction on a day-to-day basis. Most likely, the student's teachers and support staff will chart data aligned to the goals and specific objectives within the student's IEP so that, at any point in time, any member of the team can determine what skills the student is working to master, his or her level of proficiency, and the level of support he or she requires to complete a given task. Collaborative teams use this key information in their team time to direct their focus on the four PLC questions as they apply to the individual student.

Simply put, educators must commit to formative assessment. We cannot meet learner needs without regularly checking for understanding and mastery. Waiting for the end of the year, IEP, or unit of instruction is not ensuring that all students will learn. In fact, it virtually guarantees that some students will not. If we believe that all students can and will learn, we must then deeply commit to formatively monitoring student learning and adjusting instruction based on what we discover.

Yes We Can: Keys to Moving Forward

Planning standards-aligned assessments and instruction requires commitment and communication between general and special educators to ensure all students learn. Keep the following keys to moving forward in mind as you work together with your team.

- Collaborative teams should identify the assessments that will measure student learning throughout instruction (formative) as well as at the end of instruction (summative) prior to beginning a unit.

- After identifying the assessment criteria, the team can much more easily create a plan for instruction that leads to student mastery of the standards.

- Once an instructional plan is created, the team can work collaboratively to proactively identify prerequisite skills, scaffolds, and strategies that will support learners for whom the content will be challenging.

In chapter 7, we show teams how to use the data they have collected from the assessments they develop.

CHAPTER 7

PLANNING GOALS AND MONITORING PROGRESS FOR ALL LEARNERS

> *One mark of schools that make headway on the achievement gap appears to be their propensity to promote and organize conversations based in evidence of student progress.*
>
> —Judith Warren Little

As school systems, we have grown problem-solving models for students within our implementation of response to intervention legislation. Call it what you will—pyramid intervention team, student services squad, problem-solving team—nearly all schools have in place a group of specialists who have a portion of their workweek dedicated to problem solving. There are countless forms and protocols created by schools and districts to drive conversations, document interventions, and log progress-monitoring data. This support for students is critical for driving results-focused, growth-producing interventions for learners. So why does such conversation stop once students become IEP eligible? Of all students, don't our struggling learners deserve the *most* robust dialogue related to their progress and a shared commitment to problem solving?

Here's the good news. All the systems in place to support general education students can and do apply for special education students. The focus on the four critical PLC questions within team-level conversations does not change. Our mindset related to struggling learners must change, as must our commitment to a relentless pursuit of growth for all learners.

Framing IEP planning through the lens of the student's appropriate grade-level standards is critically important. One way to guarantee that a student remains in special education is to do anything other than aim for him or her to work toward the grade-level expectation. The distance between the current reality and the grade-level standard may be vast, but the educational team *must* remain committed to working toward the grade-level expectations. Please know that we are not at all arguing that we should ignore a student's current performance and proceed headlong through the curriculum. Rather, we advocate for educators following very clear steps in planning IEP goals, using the grade-level standards to guide the entire discussion. Put simply, "standards-based IEPs allow individualized instruction in pursuit of a common goal to help students with [special needs] move toward meeting the same grade-level academic standards" (Samuels, 2011, p. 8). This common goal is for all students to achieve the grade-level standard or come as close to it as is appropriate given their level of need. Although designing a standards-aligned IEP is by no means a simple process, the following logical steps can make it a successful one across content areas, grade levels, and learner profiles.

First, if a student does not have an identified deficit in a content or service area, he or she should *not* have a goal written in that domain. The educational team (teachers, related-services providers, administrators, and parents) cannot develop IEP goals based on feelings; rather, goals must align to identified data-based needs and skill deficits. This is the first step in maintaining that every student makes progress through a data-driven results orientation for our students with special needs.

Next, as educational teams, we need to consider the standards and each student's needs related to the content area. One way to easily do so is to use a preassessment before instruction begins or shortly after a brief introduction to the lesson to find out what students already know. If we think of assessment as an essential part of the instructional process, it is only natural that we would want to know what students know prior to, during, and after instruction. We've seen teams successfully approach preassessment in three ways.

1. Before starting a unit

2. As a daily end-of-period activity

3. After a brief period of initial instruction

The assessment's form can range from exit slips to student responses on whiteboards to a show of hands or observation checklists. All these methods provide opportunities for the educational team to use assessment data to make instructional decisions for learners so that the students who are already mastering the standard benefit as much as the students who may need more intensive instruction. It is imperative that teams focus on strategies that will give students meaningful learning experiences when data show that they already know the skills or concepts.

Once the educational team conducts and analyzes preassessment data, we next focus on the individual student's areas of eligibility for specialized service, specifically special education support. This conversation is driven by the team's prior work to unpack the standards. (Refer to chapter 4 for a detailed explanation of the unpacking process.) Given the student's profile and evaluation data, the educational team determines which standards to focus on and, for areas of identified deficit, defines the IEP goals in a logical progression to lead the student to grade-level proficiency. The team also determines progress-monitoring methods in order to formatively measure the student's progress. When the student has no areas of identified deficits, teachers should proceed with instruction as planned for a general education peer and use the learning progression developed in the unpacking process in chapter 4 to drive planning. The "Protocol to Focus Standards-Based IEP Goals" (page 113) and "Content Area of Focus" (page 114) worksheets in appendix A can help teams keep a record of their planning and determine next steps.

How does this then come to life in a collaborative team? Let's look at some examples. In case 1, a sixth-grade student has an identified writing disability. Specifically, the student struggles to synthesize ideas in writing and to identify ideas and evidence that support the given topic. The student is in a general education language arts class with a special education teacher as case manager of the IEP. The priority standards for an upcoming unit are identified in table 7.1 (page 86). The table also shows how the instructional decision-making plan accompanies the standards.

In case 2, a fourth-grade student has an identified learning disability in mathematics. Specifically, the student struggles with mathematics fact fluency. This deficit impacts the student's ability to apply facts when asked to problem solve. Due to the identified skill deficits, the student receives mathematics instruction in a small-group setting with a special education teacher. Table 7.2 (page 87) shows the team identifying the prioritized standards for an upcoming unit, considering the student's proficiency in each targeted standard, and then drafting the instructional decision-making plan.

Planning Goals and Monitoring Growth

Let's consider the steps an educational team planning for a seventh-grade student with reading comprehension deficits will take to address the student's academic needs. The team will need to determine the student's present level of performance, unpack standards and determine priority learning targets, and then plan goals based on the areas of identified deficit (Cathcart, Bertando, & DeRuvo, 2009).

Table 7.1: Instructional Plan to Support a Grade 6 Student's Writing Skills

Standard	Student Proficiency	Instructional Plan
W.6.1c Introduce claims and organize the reasons and evidence clearly.	Not an area of deficit. The student demonstrates proficiency.	The special education teacher, in collaboration with the sixth-grade general education language arts teachers, determines evidence of mastery and the learning progression of the standard. Instruction, assessment, and reporting align accordingly.
W.6.1b Support claims with clear reasons and relevant evidence, using credible sources and demonstrating an understanding of the topic or text.	Area of identified deficit.	The educational team uses the student's current level of performance relative to this standard to develop an IEP goal that addresses the deficit. For example: *The student will make a claim about a topic or text, providing three text-based reasons to support the claim.* The special education teacher monitors progress regularly via curriculum-based assessments aligned with short-term measurable objectives.
W.6.1c Use words, phrases, and clauses to clarify the relationships among claim(s) and reasons.	Not an area of deficit. Based on past work, the student can demonstrate proficiency with the accommodation of a graphic organizer.	The special education teacher, in collaboration with the sixth-grade general education language arts teachers, determines evidence of mastery and the learning progression of the standard. Instruction, assessment, and reporting align accordingly.
W.6.1d Establish and maintain a formal style.	Not an area of deficit.	The special education teacher, in collaboration with the sixth-grade general education language arts teachers, determines evidence of mastery and the learning progression of the standard. Instruction, assessment, and reporting align accordingly.

Source for standards: Adapted from NGA & CCSSO, 2010a.

Table 7.2: Instructional Plan to Support a Grade 4 Student's Mathematics Skills

Standard	Student Proficiency	Instructional Plan
4.NBT.B.4 Fluently add and subtract multidigit whole numbers using the standard algorithm.	Area of identified deficit.	The educational team uses the student's current level of performance relative to this standard to develop an IEP goal that addresses the deficit. For example: *The student will solve addition and subtraction problems with products to 100.* The special education teacher monitors progress regularly via curriculum-based assessments aligned with short-term measurable objectives.
4.OA.A.2 Multiply or divide to solve word problems involving multiplicative comparison, e.g., by using drawings and equations with a symbol for the unknown number to represent the problem, distinguishing multiplicative comparison from additive comparison.	Negatively impacted by the area of identified deficit. Based on past work, the student can successfully complete the task with the accommodation of a calculator, number grid, or both.	The special education teacher uses the student's current performance level relative to this standard to develop an IEP goal that addresses the deficit. For example: *The student will solve one-step real-world problems using multiplication or division within 100.* The special education teacher monitors progress regularly via curriculum-based assessments aligned with short-term measurable objectives.
4.OA.B.4 Determine whether a given whole number in the range of 1 to 100 is prime or composite. Recognize that a whole number is a multiple of each of its factors. Find all factor pairs for a whole number in the range of 1 to 100.	Not an area of deficit. Based on past work, the learner can successfully complete the task with the accommodation of a calculator, number grid, or both.	The special education teacher, in collaboration with the fourth-grade general education mathematics teachers, determines evidence of mastery and the learning progression of the standard. Instruction, assessment, and reporting align accordingly.

Source for standards: Adapted from NGA & CCSSO, 2010b.

Start With the Student's Present Levels of Performance

Assume that, for our example student, data show that to move this student toward grade-level mastery, the most important areas of concentration are reading comprehension and writing strategies with an emphasis on organization and focus.

Choose the Priority Standards That Align to the Area of Deficit

The team discusses the priority standards the seventh-grade literacy program identified and focuses on one standard the student is struggling to master (NGA & CCSSO, 2010a).

> **RI.7.1**
> Cite several pieces of textual evidence to support analysis of what the text says explicitly as well as inferences drawn from the text.

Then, the educational team writes the student's IEP goal: *Identify textual evidence to support an analysis of a given grade-level text.*

Unpack the Standard

The educational team collaborates with the other seventh-grade language arts teachers to discuss the standard. Using the unpacking process described in chapter 4, they break the standard into four component skills.

1. Cite textual evidence to support what the text explicitly states.

2. Cite textual evidence to support inferences drawn from the text.

3. Cite several pieces of related textual evidence.

4. Write an analysis of a text using textual evidence to support claims.

Analyze the Component and Prerequisite Skills

The educational team reviews the component skills and identifies the most important skill within the standard, which can be a prerequisite skill or a more concrete representation of the standard's elements. The team members will focus on these component skills as they map out the student's IEP.

Recall our example student's IEP goal to identify textual evidence to support an analysis of a given grade-level text. While the grade-level standard asks the student to identify explicit textual evidence as well as inferences drawn from the text in order to support and provide textual analysis, the essential skill that the student must first demonstrate is the ability to identify relevant textual evidence. Unless the student can demonstrate this skill, he or she cannot be expected to apply the skill to make inferences or analyze the text based on textual evidence.

Develop the Goal

The team determines what measurable indicators it will see that demonstrate the student has mastered the component skills it identified. These indicators become the measures of the IEP goal. The seventh-grade team in our example uses these indicators to refine the student's IEP goal so it is more specific and measurable. Taking the indicators into consideration, the team develops the specific goal statement to read: *By the end of the year, when given passages written at a seventh-grade text-complexity level, the student will identify at least three pieces of textual evidence he or she can use to support a written analysis of the text.*

This goal targets grade-level text as the context in which a student demonstrates the skill. Our job as educators is to scaffold the learning so that the student is able to navigate grade-level text. The student must have access to the accommodations and modifications the educational team determines and the IEP indicates, but the student must use grade-level text, except in cases where his or her foundational skills limit his or her ability to access grade-level text independently. That does not mean we don't expose him or her to complex text; rather, we would create another IEP goal targeting the skill progression necessary to remediate the deficit areas.

Write the Short-Term Objectives and Benchmarks

Once the team writes the goal statement, team members next identify the expectations for growth over the course of the goal year. Although IEP goals are not written in a SMART format, they take on many of the same attributes. These statements of incremental expectations and objectives should be measurable, align directly to the goal, and create a clear progression from the current level of performance to proficiency. The team in our example creates the following objectives for the student's IEP, beginning in September of a given school year.

- By November, the student will identify textual evidence that explicitly supports an analysis of a given grade-level text correctly in four out of five attempts, as measured by classroom discussion, daily reading journal entries, and work samples.

- By February, the student will identify textual evidence that explicitly supports inferences made related to a given grade-level text correctly in four out of five attempts, as measured by classroom discussion, daily reading journal entries, and work samples.

- By May, the student will write an analysis of a given grade-level text using explicit textual evidence correctly in two out of three attempts, as measured by work samples. (Note that the context—work samples only—changes in this objective, as it can only be measured in the student's written work. Additionally, the frequency has been changed to two out of three samples, as this type of performance task takes more time to complete than the artifacts that could serve as measures of the prior two objectives.)

- By September, the student will identify at least three pieces of textual evidence that he or she can use to support a written analysis of the text in two out of three attempts, as measured by work samples.

Thus, when the educational team convenes in September to conduct an annual review of the student's IEP, the final objective, if achieved, also indicates that the student demonstrated mastery of the identified goal.

Monitor the Goal

Using formative assessments, the team regularly collects data aligned to the objectives and benchmarks to monitor the student's progress toward the relevant objective and progress toward the goal.

Teams often struggle with ongoing goal monitoring. What if there was a construct that asks educators to problem-solve for their IEP-entitled students in the same way they do for learners participating in RTI alone? Put simply, we apply best practices in the examination of student data to ensure that these students are making the progress they need to close learning gaps. In figure 7.1, let's examine a tool that can structure these data-driven conversations for IEP-entitled students in the same way teams review data for students participating in general education interventions in the context of RTI. (See the "Individual Problem-Solving Discussion Guide" on page 115 in appendix A for a free reproducible version of figure 7.1.)

This tool compels educators to:

- Focus on one content or skill area at a time

- Focus on data relative to the content or skill area

- Move from the current status to plans for implementation and progress monitoring

While teams regularly use such an approach when discussing students' interventions, we contend that the same conversation should happen for students with IEPs with the same frequency (for instance, every six to eight weeks). This formative approach to problem solving linked to specific IEP goals will, without question, lead

Student: _____ Grade: _____

Teacher: _____ Date of Discussion: _____

Content Area of Focus: _____ Data Review Date: six to eight weeks from today

Describe the student's present levels in this content area. (Include normative data, goal-specific data, and progress-monitoring data.)

Relative to this student in this content or skill area:

1. What do we want the student to know and be able to do?

2. How will we know when the student has mastered this skill or these skills? What results will prove this to us? Use specific data indicators.

3. What do we need to know more about in order to help this student meet the targets in questions 1 and 2? What diagnostic tools are available?

4. What will we do instructionally to make sure the student meets the targets listed in questions 1 and 2?

Use the following table to plan implementation.

Plan Implementation Logistics	
Implementer	
Days or Times	
Location	
Weekly Progress Monitoring • Which measures will we use? • What other tools will we use? • Who inputs the data?	

Figure 7.1: Individual problem-solving discussion guide.

to a more focused approach to addressing student deficits in a timely fashion so that students can make progress and teams can monitor growth more effectively.

What do data-driven conversations look like when put into practice? Imagine an educational team meets to discuss a student's goal updates. Rather than simply entering the current data, the team must examine each content or skill area the goal focuses on. Within this context, the team members consider four factors.

1. The student's current performance

2. The next logical step

3. The metrics that will indicate success

4. The plan that will lead to the student reaching the target

Stretch this even further! If a student's educational team collaborates with other teachers of the same grade and content area to consider these four factors, educators will be able to:

- **Connect classroom instruction with the support provided in the special education setting:** This connection enables educators to implement academic support with fidelity, present support with consistency, and provide the preteaching and reteaching that will equip the student to be successful in the core classroom.

- **Connect academic targets with supports provided by related-services providers:** For example, if a speech pathologist is involved in team planning for a student with both reading and language deficits, the support provided in speech can be purposefully constructed to scaffold what a student needs to know and be able to do in the core classroom.

- **Connect behavioral and social-emotional goals with classroom expectations:** Imagine what will happen when every teacher working with the student plans together how to use the social work setting to support the student directly in his or her deficit areas, using scenarios and specific context that the student experiences on a daily basis. In the same way, occupational therapists, when informed about classroom expectations, can provide motor, sensory, and executive functions in ways and use tools that cross over to the different environments a student experiences.

The same process applies to learners who are learning at levels very discrepant from their grade-level expected targets. The importance of progress monitoring multiplies with students who struggle. The educational team must simply break the process down to examine even more finite skills and the aligned instructional methods that will lead to growth for those students.

Fine-Tuning Progress Monitoring for Struggling Learners

Take, for example, a structured learning class of elementary students with autism. Autism impacts the students' abilities to express their thinking, make inferences, think abstractly, and regulate their bodies to learn. In this structured learning classroom, students work in individual stations with visual supports and limited use of language in order to help students make maximum progress in mastering content. Clearly, it is essential that we identify each student's sweet spot for learning—the point where the work is challenging but not so difficult that the student becomes overstimulated or emotionally dysregulated by the stress of the rigor. The beauty of standards-aligned goal planning and aligned progress monitoring is that they allow us to continue to work toward grade-level learning with some of our most complex learners. Consider this team's plans for monitoring the students' progress in mathematics in table 7.3 and in reading in table 7.4 (page 94).

Table 7.3: Plan for Monitoring Elementary Students' Progress in Mathematics in a Structured Learning Classroom

Name	Grade	Diagnostic Identified Deficit	Aligned Weekly Progress Monitoring
Student 1	1	Number sense (mastered kindergarten standards)	Missing numbers (first-grade level)
Student 2	2	Basic facts (mastered kindergarten standards)	Computation (first-grade level)
Student 3	3	Number sense (has not yet mastered kindergarten standards)	Missing numbers (kindergarten level)
Student 4	1	Number sense (has not yet mastered kindergarten standards)	Missing numbers (kindergarten level)
Student 5	2	Basic facts (mastered first-grade standards) Problem solving (mastered first-grade standards)	Computation (second-grade level) Mathematics concepts (second-grade level)
Student 6	4	Basic facts (mastered second-grade standards) Problem solving (mastered first-grade standards)	Computation (third-grade level) Mathematics concepts (second-grade level)
Student 7	2	Basic facts (mastered first-grade standards) Problem solving (mastered first-grade standards)	Computation (second-grade level) Mathematics concepts (second-grade level)

Table 7.4: Plan for Monitoring Elementary Students' Progress in Reading in a Structured Learning Classroom

Name	Grade	Independent Reading Level	Aligned Weekly Progress Monitoring
Student 1	1	A	Running record–level A Fluency check (first-grade level)
Student 2	2	A/B	Running record–level B Fluency check (second-grade level)
Student 3	3	A	Running record–level A Fluency check (second-grade level)
Student 4	1	Read to	Letter-naming fluency check (kindergarten level) Letter-sound fluency check (kindergarten level) Sight-word recognition check (kindergarten level)
Student 5	2	F	Running record–level F Fluency check (second-grade level)
Student 6	4	D	Running record–level D Fluency check (second-grade level)
Student 7	2	F	Running record–level D Fluency check (second-grade level)

Note: Independent reading levels are based on Fountas & Pinnell, 2006.

When the team considered the area of writing, it considered the students' abilities and the impact of their disability on their abilities to write. The team determined that while measuring the total words written and measuring the correct writing sequences are essential for collecting quantitative performance data, it matched the context to the abilities of the learners. Although students are asked at times to write to *cold* (or unknown) prompts, most often students are asked to write about what they have read because this allows the team to measure writing progress. With any writing prompt, the educational team must keep in mind and attend to the students' needs for background knowledge of a concept and its embedded vocabulary before students are able to express their thoughts about it. Because reading instruction incorporates these needs and provides a foundation for students' comprehension of the text, asking students to write about what they have read gives the team meaningful data related to the students' progress in the area that is, realistically, the most challenging for its learners. This background knowledge provides the students with a scaffold to make the act of writing more attainable. Because they already know the content about which they are going to write, they can focus on getting their thoughts onto the page rather than trying to brainstorm content to write about while simultaneously turning the concepts into a written form.

In reading, writing, and mathematics, the educational team begins by reviewing the appropriate grade-level standards for each learner. The team deconstructs the standard in order to identify the subskills within the standard and then use diagnostic assessments to determine the student's current performance level. Finally, it identifies goals and aligns progress-monitoring tools that would purposefully lead the student from his or her current performance level to his or her grade-level standards.

Collecting Data Aligned to Goals

The essential point in all these examples, and when monitoring student learning, is to frequently collect data directly aligned to the goal itself. In maintaining a problem-solving mentality for all learners, we must keep in mind the essential key points.

- If a student is not making progress toward the goal, the educational team must brainstorm ways to change what is being done to better support the student.

- If, after the team adjusts instruction, the student is still not making progress, change the goal.

- In all cases, IEP teams must create a road map from current performance to the goal and grade-level learning, no matter how long the road is.

By demonstrating a consistent commitment to true problem solving for *all* students and aligning our actions with the belief that all students can and will learn, we create conditions in which each learner, regardless of disability, truly makes progress.

Yes We Can: Keys to Moving Forward

The protocols in this chapter can help general and special educators collaborate to monitor progress and use data to fine-tune students' educational plans. As you work with your team, consider the following keys to moving forward.

- IEP goals must focus on grade-level standards and each individual student's areas related to that standard and must be created collaboratively by the student's educational team.

- IEP objectives establish the plan and measurement criteria to ensure that the student makes progress toward the goal and, ideally, demonstrates mastery of the goal by the time of the IEP annual review.

- For students whose needs are so complex that achievement of the grade-level standards is not attainable, IEP goals should still reflect a functional interpretation of the standards, broken into objectives that measure progress toward the goal.

- It's not enough to write a data-driven IEP goal! Each goal must be monitored regularly in order to ensure progress and to drive changes in instruction or support if needed.

Monitoring progress, setting goals, and attending to data sometimes reveal that students aren't learning. Chapter 8 concludes part II with a look at RTI structures to help teams respond when students don't learn.

CHAPTER 8

RESPONDING WHEN STUDENTS DON'T LEARN

If the mission of the school is to ensure high levels of learning for all students, all students are entitled to participate in a system that guarantees they will receive extra time and support whenever they struggle.

—Richard DuFour

In their book *It's About Time: Planning Interventions and Extensions in Elementary School*, Austin Buffum and Mike Mattos (2015) indicate that schools must restructure their assumptions and practices around certain essential outcomes in order to achieve high levels of learning for every student. Two of these outcomes center on providing time and support for student learning. Buffum and Mattos (2015) say that one essential outcome must be that "students will be provided additional time and support to achieve these rigorous expectations" (p. 5). Second, schools need a systemwide intervention process in place to offer support that "goes beyond what an individual classroom teacher can provide" so that struggling students are guaranteed the interventions they need to learn (p. 5). The second big idea of a PLC is that "helping all students learn requires a collective and collaborative effort" (DuFour et al., 2010, p. 14), and this idea is at the forefront of successful schoolwide RTI systems. All educators must work together to decide how they will respond when students don't learn and share responsibility for every student's learning to function as an effective intervention system.

We couldn't agree more with how important these shifts are to ensuring that we close the gap for our least-advantaged students. This chapter addresses these shifts in the context of systemwide RTI. First, we'll look at how RTI grew from special education legislation and how RTI relates to PLCs. Next, we'll consider the impact of improving core instruction for all students. Then, we'll examine how collaborative teams can use tiered interventions to support students with special needs.

Examining Response to Intervention Legislation

When the Individuals With Disabilities Education Act was reauthorized in 2004, *RTI* became a buzzword. While the many purposes of RTI include focusing on early intervention, improving the quality of instruction, and potentially avoiding the need for special education services, these facets were often overlooked because many people had the impression that RTI applied only to special education, as it was buried in special education law. RTI was only discussed in depth in special education and related-services workshops and conferences where the reauthorization took center stage. Special education administrators, special education teachers, related-services personnel, and special education attorneys dissected the language and began the arduous task of interpretation and implementation. The realization that RTI was a piece of general education legislation embedded into special education law grew gradually depending on the speed with which each state issued its own guidance. While some states issued very specific guidance quickly, others are just now providing state-level parameters.

Recall that PLCs require a system of intervention to answer the third and fourth critical questions, How will we respond when some students do not learn? and How will we respond when some students already know it? In the context of PLCs, RTI offers a pyramid of systematic, schoolwide interventions that:

> ensures every student in every course or grade level will receive additional time and support for learning as soon as he or she experiences difficulty in acquiring essential knowledge and skills. The intervention occurs during the school day and students are required rather than invited to devote the extra time and secure the extra support for learning. (DuFour et al., 2010, pp. 99–100)

The following core principals of RTI legislation will support us in making connections to the critical work of PLCs (Mellard & National Research Center on Learning Disabilities, 2006).

- Unequivocally believing that we can effectively teach all students and all students can learn

- Focusing early intervention and prevention in academic, behavioral, and social-emotional arenas

- Universally screening all students for academic, behavioral, and social-emotional indicators of success

- Using a problem-solving and problem-analysis methodology

- Using research-based, scientifically validated interventions and instructional practices that are implemented with fidelity

- Monitoring progress of students' responses to intervention on an ongoing basis

- Practicing data-based decision making at all levels of the process

- Using assessments for screening, diagnostics, and progress monitoring in a data-based decision-making process and using multitiered systems with increasing levels of intensity and support

All of this means creating a robust core curriculum that meets student needs through a cycle of instruction that allows teachers to formatively assess and intervene before moving on. Through the universal screening process, some students are identified as at-risk and do require supplementary instruction and support in addition to core instruction. A few students are identified as needing more intensive small-group or individualized intervention to supplement the core curriculum. Essentially, RTI enables educators to target instructional interventions aligned to students' very specific needs early and as soon as they become evident.

From "Wait to Fail" to Success for All

Formerly, the system could be referred to as a "wait to fail" system since the most intensive interventions available (often special education) would only be provided once a large, statistically significant gap existed. This new, more immediate early intervention model is critical to students' success. RTI allows special and general educators to share the responsibility for the learning of *all* students and creates a uniform education system that focuses on the successes of all.

In "A Cultural, Linguistic, and Ecological Framework for Response to Intervention With English Language Learners," authors Julie Esparza Brown and Jennifer Doolittle (2008) state that "first, the universal screening and progress monitoring allow for comparison of students to other or 'true' peers in their local cohort rather than to national norms" (p. 70). While U.S. norms have a place in our data discussions, local norms align to local expectations. Second, Brown and Doolittle (2008) continue, "An effective RTI model requires collaboration among all educators, providing increased opportunities for professional dialogue, peer coaching, and the creation of instructional models integrating the best practices of the various fields of [educational] related services"(p. 70). Put another way, the successful implementation of RTI requires a highly collaborative culture where teams of education professionals relentlessly focus on student learning and student work in order to improve outcomes for students. Third, Brown and Doolittle (2008) emphasize an effective RTI model is essential so that "students who are struggling can be identified early and supported before falling too far behind in the system" (p. 71).

Sound familiar? RTI core principles and the PLC framework both simultaneously require a highly collaborative culture where there is collective responsibility for the learning of *all* students. In this culture, educators agree on what all students should know and be able to do and have a results orientation where data drive instruction and intervention. This system is fluid and allows educators to respond at all tiers with more time and intensity when students are not learning. Now, let's look at how collaborative teams in PLCs can use RTI to ensure all students learn, close the learning gap, and remove the barriers between general and special education.

Making Connections Between RTI and PLCs

RTI supports answering PLC critical question 3, How will we respond when some students do not learn? Figure 8.1 illustrates this important concept and that collaborative teams must engage in the ongoing critical work of a PLC at the core of a robust instructional cycle in Tier 1 in order for student outcomes to improve. It will not be enough to develop elaborate systems of intervention at Tiers 2 and 3 if this is not the case. Without continuous commitment to PLC work in Tier 1, improvement will not be significant or sustainable.

The ongoing work of systems to answer the four critical questions in a cycle of continuous improvement betters outcomes for all students based on what is happening in the classroom every day. As that work becomes richer and deeper, teams see a steady improvement in student results at Tier 1. Simultaneously, the percentage of students for whom educators must develop Tiers 2 and 3 interventions will steadily decrease as more students successfully master content and learning targets due to a more robust cycle of instruction at Tier 1 (figure 8.2).

As we can see, when collaborative teams sharpen their focus on core instruction at Tier 1, the number of students who require more intensive intervention at Tiers 2 and 3 may be reduced significantly.

Improving Core Instruction to Close the Gap

For some schools and districts, especially those new to implementing a systemwide RTI process, the gap between students at Tier 1 and Tiers 2 and 3 reveals inadequate core instruction. For example, consider the school whose data are represented in figure 8.3 (page 102). We contend that if 68 percent of this school's students are meeting expectations as the result of classroom instruction at Tier 1, it is not feasible for this school—or any school or system—to create Tiers 2 and 3 interventions for 32 percent of its population. Our experience is that systems collapse under the weight

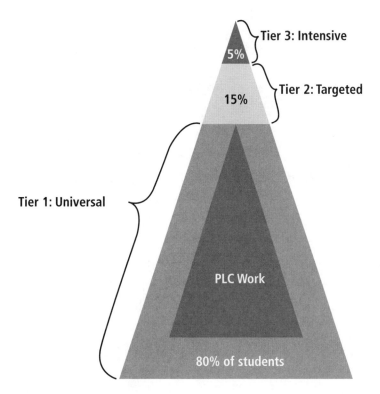

Figure 8.1: PLC work and RTI.

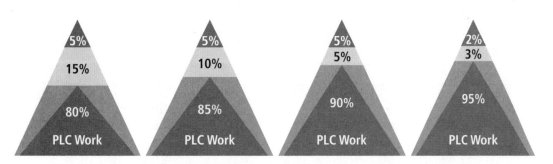

Figure 8.2: Distribution of students by RTI tier when PLC work in Tier 1 core instruction deepens over time.

of the disproportionate number of students requiring more intensive interventions. When human and fiscal resources are limited, we assert it is not a particularly feasible goal that 80 percent of students should be meeting core instruction as the familiar triangle graphic (such as that depicted by figure 8.1) suggests. Schools and systems that allocate the vast majority of their time and resources into developing, implementing, and monitoring Tiers 2 and 3 are likely exhausted and frustrated. Without

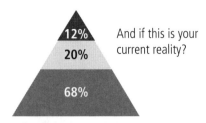

And if this is your current reality?

Is it feasible to develop systems to support 32 percent
of your student population in Tiers 2 and 3?

Figure 8.3: Disproportionate distribution of students by RTI tiers.

significant time, attention, and resources allocated to continuous improvement of
core instruction in Tier 1, the effort to support all learners is unsustainable. Unless
there is a relentless commitment to improving the instructional practices of every
teacher, creating a more robust cycle of instruction, the percentage of students needing
support at Tiers 2 and 3 will not decrease and overall outcomes will likely not change
significantly, particularly for your students who struggle the most.

If a school or a district already started on the PLC journey at the time RTI legislation became federal law, the connection between new RTI legislation and the
school's or district's current work may have seemed nebulous. That is, until the school
or district closely examined the connections and where the new, tiered approach to
intervention connected to its PLC's continuous focus on answering the four critical
questions.

When we, as authors, are asked to work with schools and districts across the United
States on implementing PLCs and on embedding systems of intervention, we commonly find that schools and districts dedicate significant resources to providing Tier
2 and Tier 3 interventions, yet they do not see much, if any, improvement. They have
paid little attention to developing high-performing collaborative teams, ensuring a
guaranteed and viable curriculum, and implementing a balanced and coherent system
of assessment. This aha moment typically leads such schools and districts to action
planning for high-quality Tier 1 instruction for all students. Implementing RTI
without doing the work of a PLC is not lasting or effective. Recognizing the value
of PLC work and taking action to provide high-quality core instruction at Tier 1 are
the first steps on the road to sustainable improvement.

Connecting RTI and PLC Practices for Special Education Students

The connections between RTI and PLC practices are particularly important for
special education students and students who may, in the past, have been identified

as needing special education services but who can now succeed with tiered intervention. RTI and PLC practices connect general and special education in unmistakable ways and require high levels of collaboration around the learning of all. When both RTI and PLC are implemented with fidelity in schools, the entire system embraces the responsibility for the success of special education students, leading to access to:

- Classroom or grade-level intervention at Tier 1 that is closely connected to targets currently being taught

- Tiers 2 and 3 intervention in areas not identified as areas of disabilities

- Potential Tiers 2 and 3 intervention in areas of disability as deemed appropriate by the problem-solving team

- Special education and related services along the continuum of the least- to most-restrictive learning environments for areas of identified disability

- Targeted skill-deficit remediation in areas not identified as areas of disability (Tiers 2 and 3) and in areas identified as areas of disability (special education)

- A fuller range of highly qualified adults

Let's dig a little deeper into the shifts in access and practice that make the list possible.

Delving Into Shifts in Access and Practice

In our work with schools, we find that when we question how a system of intervention is accessed by students who are already special education eligible, the response is often concerning and, at times, illogical. Replies often fall into two different categories. The first one speaks to the reality of a school taking collective responsibility for the learning of all students, and that is, "They already get help through special education services" or "That is special education's responsibility." These responses imply the special education team is responsible for fixing issues with special education students. After all, the team members provide special education minutes through the IEP. The expectation is that the special education team somehow intervenes. This is often the case, regardless of what a student's eligibility for services might be or what the adverse effects of the disability might be.

The second common response is that special education students are pulled out of the mainstream classroom during core content instruction to receive specialized help and related services, or during identified classroom or grade-level intervention time when students get differentiated intervention and enrichment on targets currently being taught before moving on to the next unit of instruction. Thus, students who most need them are missing initial instruction and the intervention on targets being taught in Tier 1. In addition, the grade-level team or the problem-solving team often does not discuss special education students; rather, those discussions are left to the special education team. This raises concerns on two fronts. It reinforces the notion that it is solely the responsibility of special education to teach and support eligible students. Also, it restricts access to highly qualified teachers in the system who provide intervention. When special education students receive high-quality special education services *and* access intervention through the tiers—where all professionals are collaborating to support their growth—they gain an equitable education that is the best pathway to closing the gap. (See chapter 6 for a comprehensive approach to conversations that demonstrates a results orientation for our most at-risk students.)

In a setting where educators take collective responsibility, the grade-level or content-alike team treats a special education–eligible student the same way it does any other student who struggles in the core. In Tier 1, individual teachers collect formative data, the team reviews common formative data, and the team discusses instructional strategies that work well and those that are less successful. Team members identify students who need intervention and then create a plan to intervene either collectively or as individuals on the target they are teaching. In a PLC where collaborative concepts are deeply embedded, the special educator is included on the team in a meaningful way. Teachers do not set aside the data of special education students when designing instruction but rather discuss, design, and differentiate instruction inclusive of all student data. In fact, if students truly have full access to the entire continuum of supports available, multiple teams discuss their needs collaboratively and address:

- General education classroom teachers in their cycle of instruction

- Grade-level teams that share data and design Tier 1 interventions

- The problem-solving team when data suggest students may be eligible for Tier 2 or Tier 3 intervention and then to monitor progress

- Special education and related-services teams that are monitoring progress toward IEP goals and objectives

In chapter 7, we ask the question, "Of all students, don't our struggling learners deserve the *most* robust dialogue related to their progress and a shared commitment to problem solving?" The answer is yes! Table 8.1 outlines the shifts needed to support this affirmative answer.

In chapter 1, we noted that 80 to 85 percent of all special education–eligible students do not have a significant cognitive disability and that their disability is not correlated to IQ in any way. Thus, access to interventions in the way that we suggest not only makes sense but must become non-negotiable in every system. Not giving students full access can only be considered educational malpractice. In addition,

Table 8.1: Some Significant Shifts in Access and Practice

From . . .	To . . .
The student with an IEP struggles in the classroom, and the teacher notifies the special education case manager.	The teacher collaborates with the grade-level team, which includes the special education teacher, to support the student.
The student receives support from special education in areas of disability.	Through problem solving, the team may determine that a student would benefit from accessing Tier 2 or Tier 3 interventions in the area of disability, in addition to special education support.
The student with reading comprehension difficulty struggles with mathematics targets, so the teacher notifies the special education case manager.	Based on formative data, the teacher includes the student in Tier 1 intervention for mathematics and refers the student to the problem-solving team if data need to be reviewed for inclusion in Tiers 2 and 3 interventions.
The student with an IEP has underlying skill deficits, so the special education teacher or related-services personnel pull the student from the classroom during core content instruction or during classroom or grade-level intervention time.	The student remains in the classroom for all core content instruction and is included in all Tier 1 intervention time. Skill deficits in areas of disability are targeted during resource minutes or another specifically designated time.
The special education teacher works with special education–eligible students only.	The special education teacher, during Tier 1 intervention time, may work with all students who have the same need, regardless of eligibility.
Special education case managers review the data of special education students, and general education teachers review the data of general education students.	Collaborative teams review the data of all students in their classrooms, and special education case managers maintain a problem-solving process with special education students by reviewing progress-monitoring data at least every six weeks to determine appropriate next steps.

students whose eligibility falls into a category with lower incidence rates must be monitored frequently in order to determine whether access to any of the levels of intervention may be appropriate. It should not be uncommon for students whose needs require that a significant portion of their day be spent in a self-contained setting for, say, autism, to access other, less restrictive settings for areas of strength. As they do so, access to the continuum of interventions provided associated with that less restrictive setting should be made available.

Yes We Can: Keys to Moving Forward

Improving core instruction at Tier 1 deeply benefits all students. When students don't learn, however, it is important for general and special educators to collaborate and support the more intensive interventions those students may require. As you work with your team, consider the following keys to moving forward.

- Shift mindset to ensure that all students have access to all levels of support available in a school, regardless of eligibility.

- Devote significant time and resources to developing a more robust cycle of instruction in Tier 1 (which includes all special education self-contained or instructional classrooms).

- Develop and implement very clear criteria and processes for accessing Tiers 2 and 3 interventions locally.

- Be more flexible in utilizing highly qualified professionals to support all learners.

Once teams have made an unwavering commitment to the shifts, only then will they begin to see a steady improvement in outcomes for all learners that results in closing the gap between general education students and those with special needs.

Final Thoughts

Our greatest hope is that this book does not fall into the hands of special educators alone. General education teachers, school support personnel, school-level administrators, and district-level administrators must commit to working together. Improving the outcomes for students with special needs cannot be the sole responsibility of special educators but must be the responsibility of the entire system. The significant shifts in culture and structure required to make this a reality can, in our experience, best be done through the ongoing collaborative work of a PLC. This community, however, must welcome all of those responsible for students' success so all educators may benefit from the rich conversations that teams engage in during their time together. It is time to remove the barriers that continue to keep general and special education separate.

We recognize that the concepts, suggestions, and protocols this book outlines may challenge many educators' thinking. What everyone does agree on and what data support are that we continue to see large gaps in achievement between special and general education students. Those gaps lead to longitudinal societal disadvantages that are well documented. With *Yes We Can!*, we have attempted to leave you with action-oriented practices that you can implement no matter where you are in your journey toward improved outcomes for *all* students. We don't contend that the work is easy. In fact, it is messy and fraught with potential barriers that will require continuous reflection and problem solving. However, doing nothing equates to educational malpractice and ensures that nothing changes for the students you serve. And in our seventy collective years as educators, we have rarely met a colleague who is okay with that.

Appendix A: Reproducibles

A ppendix A contains free reproducible versions of many of the tools mentioned throughout the book. Visit **go.solution-tree.com/PLCbooks** to download these free reproducibles.

Simple as 1, 2, 3: The Prioritizing Process

The Simple as 1, 2, 3 process provides teams with a step-by-step plan for developing priority standards.

To prioritize step 1, individuals make initial choices based on criteria. Each team member makes an initial assessment of what standards should be prioritized by studying the three criteria Douglas Reeves (2002) outlines: (1) endurance, (2) leverage, and (3) readiness for the next level of learning.

> The standard must meet one or more of these criteria:
>
> 1. **Endurance** means that the standard reflects learning that will be important now and for a long time to come. For example, in mathematics, a deep understanding of place value is important for students beyond grade school. It isn't something that they will need to know only for a grade level or for a summative assessment.
>
> 2. **Leverage** refers to learning that has cross-curricular implications; something that is taught in one subject but used in another subject. For example, we teach students about unit rate in mathematics but use that concept to solve problems in physical science classes.
>
> 3. **Readiness for the next level of learning** identifies prerequisite skills. For example, students are taught letter and sound recognition in early literacy, which are important skills when learning to read. Students who don't learn letter and sound recognition have a difficult time with future reading skills. (as cited in Bailey, Jakicic, & Spiller, 2014, p. 49)

After analyzing and discussing these three criteria, each team member reviews the full list of unit standards created in action step 1 and is given no more than ten minutes to make her or his initial individual choices regarding what standards should be prioritized. The team member will be applying professional knowledge and judgment to mark or highlight the standards she or he believes meet one or more of the criteria. It is important that this silent time to think is provided to foster individual accountability and avoid group think. Special educators should be full participants in this process if they teach the content and should approach this process with typical grade-level expectations in mind. While they will naturally consider their students' current gaps, the process of determining priority should not be based on individual student considerations. Priority should be based on high expectations for all grade-level students.

Prioritizing step 2 means developing an initial list of priority standards. Teams come to initial conclusions regarding the priority standards list. Teachers share their individual choices using a round-robin structure. One person begins by identifying a standard he or she chose as priority, giving an explanation for his or her choice. Explanations should include how the person's choice reflects the three criteria of endurance, leverage, and readiness for the next level of learning. What teams do not want to hear is, "I chose this standard because it is something we already do and it will be easy for students to learn." As each team member shares, others reveal if they also marked that standard and give their explanation and thinking. It is unlikely that there will be full agreement on a particular standard, but if there is, celebrate! If not, the discussion that ensues is often very robust and enlightening. Teachers discover understandings and misunderstandings about the standards that they may not have thought about before. In order for this conversation to be productive and include all voices, determine ahead of time how the team will handle a lack of consensus. The team may decide to develop or use a previously developed list of behavioral norms to guide these professional debates. This process continues until all team members are satisfied with their initial list of priority standards.

Prioritizing step 3 entails reviewing other sources of information to make final decisions. In this step, team members gather information that will be helpful in making a final decision regarding what students need to know and be able to do. A review of the previous and subsequent grade-level, subject-area, and course standards is critical in determining appropriate vertical alignment. For instance, in reviewing the subsequent grade-level standards for mathematics, the team may find that demonstrating a strong understanding of the division of fractions will be necessary for students to be able to master the next learning level. If the team members prioritized division of fractions, they have taken a positive step toward aligning standards vertically. If not, the team will need to consider whether to add the standard to its prioritized list. Whenever possible, consider sharing your initial set of priority standards with the grade levels or courses prior to and after your grade level or course (for example, third grade shares with second grade and fourth grade) to properly ensure strong vertical alignment. Teams can facilitate this process by sharing the list of priority standards electronically and asking the team members to provide feedback, or by having at least one team member from each grade level or course come together to discuss the vertical progression. If the entire school or district is participating in this process, the vertical alignment component becomes its own step, and teams analyze full priority lists from grade to grade. When engaging in smaller-scale work, this is not always feasible.

Team members will also want to pay attention to information they have from accountability assessments, such as state end-of-year tests. This information may include test blueprints, released assessment items and practice tests, or other documents indicating the amount of emphasis placed on certain standards for state assessment purposes. Team members may decide to add other documents to consider, depending on which documents guide teaching and learning in their setting.

Sources: Bailey, K., Jakicic, C., & Spiller, J. (2014). Collaborating for success with the Common Core: A toolkit for Professional Learning Communities at Work. *Bloomington, IN: Solution Tree Press; Reeves, D. (2002).* The leader's guide to standards: A blueprint for educational equity and excellence. *San Francisco: Jossey-Bass.*

Unpacking Document

The "Unpacking Document" reproducible gives teams a structure for each step of the unpacking process. We have found that most teams recreate this document electronically, making it easier for them to access the information after the process is complete.

Standards:				
What Will Students Do (Skills or Verbs)	**With What Knowledge or Concept**	**Level of Thinking or Type of Assessment**	**Vocabulary**	**Scaffolds or Supports**
Learning Progression:				

Protocol to Focus Standards-Based IEP Goals

This tool can be used to determine standards-aligned IEP goals based on grade-level standards and areas of identified deficit. Please refer to chapter 7 for details.

Follow these directions to identify areas of deficit and plan next steps.

1. In the Standard column, identify the standards assessed. List one standard per row.

2. In the Student Proficiency column, use the assessment data to identify any areas of deficit and eligibility.

3. In the Instructional Plan column, use the data in the Student Proficiency column to guide planning. In the case of no identified deficits, indicate that instruction will proceed following the learning progression planned for general education students. In the case of identified deficits and eligibility, develop IEP goals to address the skill deficits in a logical progression to lead the student to grade-level proficiency, and determine progress-monitoring methods in order to formatively measure student progress.

Standard	Student Proficiency	Instructional Plan

Content Area of Focus

Standard	Student Proficiency	Instructional Plan

Individual Problem-Solving Discussion Guide

This tool can be used to focus team discussion related to student progress for learners who are IEP eligible as well as those participating in general education interventions. Please refer to chapter 7 for details.

Student: _____   Grade: _____

Teacher: _____   Date of Discussion: _____

Content Area of Focus: _____   Data Review Date: six to eight weeks from today

Describe the student's present levels in this content area. (Include normative data, goal-specific data, and progress-monitoring data.)

Relative to this student in this content or skill area:

1. What do we want the student to know and be able to do?

2. How will we know when the student has mastered this skill or these skills? What results will prove this to us? Use specific data indicators.

3. What do we need to know more about in order to help this student meet the targets in questions 1 and 2? What diagnostic tools are available?

4. What will we do instructionally to make sure the student meets the targets listed in questions 1 and 2?

page 1 of 2

Use the following table to plan implementation.

Plan Implementation Logistics	
Implementer	
Days or Times	
Location	
Weekly Progress Monitoring • Which measures will be used? • What other tools will be used? • Who inputs the data?	

Appendix B: Glossary

Common Core State Standards (CCSS).

> The Common Core is a set of high-quality academic standards in mathematics and English language arts/literacy. These learning goals outline what a student should know and be able to do at the end of each grade level. The standards were created to ensure that all students graduate from high school with the skills and knowledge necessary to succeed in college, career, and life, regardless of where they live. (NGA & CCSSO, n.d.a)

Common formative assessment. Assessments for learning administered to all students in the same grade level or course several times during a unit of study, semester, or year. Participating teachers collaboratively design items, and results are analyzed in collaborative teams in order to differentiate instruction (Ainsworth & Viegut, 2006).

Discrepancy model. The IQ-achievement discrepancy model is:

> The traditional method used to determine if a student has a learning disability and needs special education services. The discrepancy model is based on the concept of the normal curve, and assesses whether a substantial difference, or discrepancy, exists between a student's scores on an individualized test of general intelligence (that is, an IQ test, such as WISC-IV) and his or her scores obtained for one or more areas of academic achievement (such as the Woodcock-Johnson Achievement Test). The accepted criteria to identify a student as having a learning disability using the IQ-achievement discrepancy is a difference of at least two standard deviations (30 points). (IRIS Center, 2015)

Formative assessment. Assessments that gather information regarding student learning of targets that are currently being taught. By using formative assessment, teachers check student learning along the way so that those who haven't yet learned the concepts are provided with additional time and support while instruction is ongoing (Bailey et al., 2014).

Four critical questions of a PLC. Questions that guide collaboration in a PLC:

> (1) What is it we want each student to learn?, (2) How will we know when each student has learned?, (3) How will we respond when some of our students do not learn?, and (4) How will we enrich

and extend the learning for students who are proficient? (DuFour, DuFour, & Eaker, 2008, pp. 183–184)

Guaranteed and viable curriculum. *Guaranteed* means that every student is provided with the opportunity to learn a core curriculum that allows him or her the probability of success in school. *Viable* means that schools make sure that the necessary time is available and protected so students will be able to learn the guaranteed curriculum (Marzano, 2003).

Individuals With Disabilities Education Act (IDEA). The Education for All Handicapped Children Act (Public Law 94-142) enacted by the United States Congress in 1975 guaranteed a free, appropriate public education to children with disabilities in every state in the United States. When amended in 1997, this act became the Individuals With Disabilities Education Act. It was amended once again in December 2004 with regulations published in August 2006 (part B for school-aged children) and in September 2011 (part C for babies and toddlers).

Learning targets. Increments of learning—steps of knowledge or concepts and skills—that build on each other and culminate in attainment of the standard. In other words, learning targets are the *knows*, *understands*, and *able to dos* that a student will demonstrate by the end of instruction (Bailey et al., 2014).

Professional learning community (PLC). "An ongoing process in which educators work collaboratively in recurring cycles of collective inquiry and action research to achieve better results for the students they serve" (DuFour et al., 2010, p. 11).

Pyramid of interventions. A multitiered system of intervention in which:

> A schoolwide plan ensures every student in every course or grade level will receive additional time and support for learning as soon as they experience difficulty in acquiring essential knowledge and skills. The intervention occurs during the school day and students are required rather than invited to devote the extra time and secure the extra support for learning. A system of intervention means that providing this support for students is a collective, schoolwide responsibility rather than the sole responsibility of the individual teacher. (DuFour et al., 2010, pp. 99–100)

Scaffolding. A process that supports students solving tasks or achieving goals that they would not normally be able to solve without assistance (Wood, Bruner, & Ross, 1976).

School culture. "The assumptions, beliefs, values, and habits that constitute the norm for the school and guide the work of the educators within it" (DuFour et al., 2008, p. 21).

Standard or learning standard or objective. A written description of what students are expected to know and be able to do at a specific stage of their education. Learning standards describe educational objectives—for example, what students should have learned by the end of a course, grade level, or grade span—but they do not describe any particular teaching practice, curriculum, or assessment method.

Students with special needs. Terminology used consistently throughout this book to describe students eligible for special education services via individualized education programs (IEPs). The following terms are often used interchangeably to describe students with special needs: *special education students, individualized education program–entitled students, students with IEPs, students with identified special needs, special education–eligible students,* and *students with disabilities.*

Summative assessment. Assessments that measure how well students have learned the concepts *after* the teacher has finished instruction (Bailey et al., 2014). It is important to note that what determines whether any given assessment is summative or formative is how it is used. A more summative assessment can be used in a more formative way if the evidence of student learning derived from the assessment is used to provide additional time and support for students.

Three big ideas of a PLC. Ideas that guide the work of a PLC:

> (1) The purpose of our school is to ensure all students learn at high levels; (2) Helping all students learn requires a collaborative and collective effort; and (3) To assess our effectiveness in helping all students learn, we must focus on results—evidence of student learning—and use results to inform and improve our professional practice and respond to students who need intervention or enrichment. (DuFour et al., 2010, p. 14)

Tier 1. Intervention provided to *all* students closely tied to targets currently being taught in the classroom in a robust cycle of instruction. This tier represents a school's core instructional program (DuFour, 2015).

Tier 2. In addition to tier 1, more time and intensity are provided to some students who demonstrate a pattern of struggling to master multiple grade-level targets or demonstrate underlying skill deficits, either of which acts as a barrier to demonstrating grade-level proficiency. This tier targets skills and knowledge needed to succeed the following year and beyond (DuFour, 2015).

Tier 3. Provided to a few students to address underlying skill deficits (as determined by additional diagnostics) that impact learning across subject areas. Tier 3 focuses on the development of universal skills of learning that can only be developed over time. These services must be provided in addition to a student's access to essential grade-level curriculum, not in place of it (DuFour, 2015). Criteria for this level of support are defined locally. Tier 3 interventions are unique to every student and driven by an individual problem solving process.

Unpacking or unwrapping. A strategy that enables collaborative teams "to achieve collective clarity and agreement regarding specific learning targets contained within the standards" (Bailey & Jakicic, 2012, p. 79). Chapter 4 discusses this strategy extensively. We use the terms *unpacking* and *unwrapping* interchangeably.

References and Resources

ACT. (2006). *Reading between the lines: What the ACT reveals about college readiness in reading.* Iowa City, IA: Author. Accessed at www.act.org/research/policymakers /pdf/reading_report.pdf on December 9, 2015.

Ainsworth, L., & Viegut, D. (2006). *Common formative assessments: How to connect standards-based instruction and assessment.* Thousand Oaks, CA: Corwin Press.

Allen, R. (2012). Supporting struggling students with academic rigor: A conversation with author and educator Robyn Jackson. *Education Update, 54*(8), 3–5. Accessed at www.ascd.org/publications/newsletters/education-update/aug12/vol54/num08 /Support-Struggling-Students-with-Academic-Rigor.aspx on July 23, 2015.

Armstrong, T. (2012). *Neurodiversity in the classroom: Strength-based strategies to help students with special needs succeed in school and life.* Alexandria, VA: Association for Supervision and Curriculum Development.

Bailey, K., & Jakicic, C. (2012). *Common formative assessment: A toolkit for Professional Learning Communities at Work.* Bloomington, IN: Solution Tree Press.

Bailey, K., Jakicic, C., & Spiller, J. (2014). *Collaborating for success with the Common Core: A toolkit for Professional Learning Communities at Work.* Bloomington, IN: Solution Tree Press.

Bambrick-Santoyo, P. (2010). *Driven by data: A practical guide to improve instruction.* San Francisco: Jossey-Bass.

Barth, R. S. (1991). Restructuring schools: Some questions for teachers and principals. *Phi Delta Kappan, 73*(2), 123–128.

Bell, R. (1990, November 28). Tried-and-true educational methods aren't true to the special needs of prison inmates. *Chicago Tribune,* sect. 1, p. 23.

Blanchard, K., Carlos, J. P., & Randolph, A. (2001). *Empowerment takes more than a minute* (2nd ed.). San Francisco: Berrett-Koehler.

Bradley, R., Danielson, L., & Hallahan, D. P. (Eds.). (2002). *Identification of learning disabilities: Research to practice.* Mahwah, NJ: Erlbaum.

Brown, J. E., & Doolittle, J. (2008). A cultural, linguistic, and ecological framework for response to intervention with English language learners. *Teaching Exceptional Children, 40*(5), 66–72.

Buffum, A., & Mattos, M. (Eds.). (2015). *It's about time: Planning interventions and extensions in elementary school.* Bloomington, IN: Solution Tree Press.

Buffum, A., Mattos, M., & Weber, C. (2009). *Pyramid response to intervention: RTI, professional learning communities, and how to respond when kids don't learn.* Bloomington, IN: Solution Tree Press.

Buffum, A., Mattos, M., & Weber, C. (2012). *Simplifying response to intervention: Four essential guiding principles.* Bloomington, IN: Solution Tree Press.

Caruana, V. (2015). Accessing the Common Core standards for students with learning disabilities: Strategies for writing standards-based IEP goals. *Preventing School Failure: Alternative Education for Children and Youth, 59*(4), 237–243.

Cathcart, M., Bertando, S., & DeRuvo, S. L. (2009). Infusing IEPs with content. *The Special EDge, 23*(1), insert.

Childress, S. M., Doyle, D. P., & Thomas, D. A. (2009). *Leading for equity: The pursuit of excellence in Montgomery County Public Schools.* Cambridge, MA: Harvard Education Press.

Clifton, D. O., & Anderson, E. (2002). *StrengthsQuest: Discover and develop your strengths in academics, career, and beyond.* Washington, DC: Gallup.

Clifton, D. O., & Harter, J. K. (2003). Investing in strengths. In K. S. Cameron, J. E. Dutton, & R. E. Quinn (Eds.), *Positive organizational scholarship: Foundations of a new discipline* (pp. 111–121). San Francisco: Berrett-Koehler.

Cortiella, C., & Horowitz, S. H. (2014). *The state of learning disabilities: Facts, trends and emerging issues* (3rd ed.). New York: National Center for Learning Disabilities. Accessed at www.ncld.org/wp-content/uploads/2014/11/2014-State-of-LD.pdf on December 9, 2015.

Denton, C. A., Vaughn, S., & Fletcher, J. M. (2003). Bringing research-based practice in reading intervention to scale. *Learning Disabilities Research and Practice, 18*(3), 201–211.

Diamond, K. E., Justice, L. M., Siegler, R. S., & Snyder, P. A. (2013, July). *Synthesis of IES research on early intervention and early childhood education.* Washington, DC: National Center for Special Education Research, U.S. Department of Education. Accessed at https://ies.ed.gov/ncser/pubs/20133001/pdf/20133001.pdf on December 10, 2015.

Douglass, F. (1985). The significance of emancipation in the West Indies: Speech presented at Canandaigua, New York, August 3, 1857. In J. W. Blassingame (Ed.), *The Frederick Douglass papers, series one, vol. 3: 1855–63* (p. 204). New Haven, CT: Yale University Press: (Original work published 1857)

Duckworth, A. L., Peterson, C., Matthews, M. D., & Kelly, D. R. (2007). Grit: Perseverance and passion for long-term goals. *Journal of Personality and Social Psychology, 92*(6), 1087–1101.

DuFour, R. (2015). *In praise of American educators: And how they can become even better.* Bloomington, IN: Solution Tree Press.

DuFour, R., DuFour, R., & Eaker, R. (2008). *Revisiting Professional Learning Communities at Work: New insights for improving schools.* Bloomington, IN: Solution Tree Press.

DuFour, R., DuFour, R., Eaker, R., & Many, T. (2010). *Learning by doing: A handbook for Professional Learning Communities at Work* (2nd ed.). Bloomington, IN: Solution Tree Press.

Engage New York. (2012). *Instructional shifts for the Common Core.* Accessed at www.engageny.org/resource/common-core-shifts on August 19, 2015.

Fountas, I. C., & Pinnell, G. S. (2006). *Leveled books (K–8): Matching texts to readers for effective teaching.* Portsmouth, NH: Heinemann.

Fullan, M. (2000). The three stories of education reform. *Phi Delta Kappan, 81*(8), 581–584.

Gersten, R., Fuchs, L. S., Williams, J. P., & Baker, S. (2001). Teaching reading comprehension strategies to students with learning disabilities: A review of research. *Review of Educational Research, 71*(2), 279–320.

Gong, B., & Simpson, M. A. (2005). *Kids in the gap?: Academic performance and disability characteristics of special education students.* Dover, NH: Center for Assessment.

Individuals With Disabilities Education Act, 20 U.S.C. § 1400 (2004).

International Center for Leadership in Education. (2011, February). *Fewer, clearer, higher Common Core State Standards: Implications for students receiving special education services* [White paper]. Rexford, NY: Author. Accessed at http://teacher.scholastic.com/products/scholastic-achievement-partners/downloads/SpecialED_CCSS.pdf on December 10, 2015.

IRIS Center. (2015). *RTI (part 1)* [STAR Legacy module]. Nashville, TN: IRIS Center, Peabody College, Vanderbilt University. Accessed at http://iris.peabody.vanderbilt.edu/module/rti01-overview on December 10, 2015.

Jackson, R. R., & Lambert, C. (2010). *How to support struggling students.* Alexandria, VA: Association for Supervision and Curriculum Development.

Kaldenberg, E. R., Watt, S. J., & Therrien, W. J. (2015). Reading instruction in science for students with learning disabilities: A meta-analysis. *Learning Disability Quarterly, 38*(3), 160–173.

Little, J. W. (1990). The persistence of privacy: Autonomy and initiative in teachers' professional relations. *Teachers College Record, 91*(4), 509–536.

Little, J. W. (2006, December). *Professional community and professional development in the learning-centered school* [Working paper]. Washington, DC: National Education Association. Accessed at www.nea.org/assets/docs/HE/mf_pdreport.pdf on August 24, 2015.

Lyon, G. R., Fletcher, J. M., Shaywitz, S. E., Shaywitz, B. A., Torgesen, J. K., Wood, F. B., et al. (2001). Rethinking learning disabilities. In C. E. Finn Jr., A. J. Rotherham, & C. R. Hokanson Jr. (Eds.), *Rethinking special education for a new century* (pp. 259–287). Washington, DC: Thomas B. Fordham Foundation.

Marzano, R. J. (2003). *What works in schools: Translating research into action.* Alexandria, VA: Association for Supervision and Curriculum Development.

Marzano, R. J. (2004). *Building background knowledge for academic achievement: Research on what works in schools.* Alexandria, VA: Association for Supervision and Curriculum Development.

Marzano, R. J. (2012, August). *Marzano levels of school effectiveness* [White paper]. Centennial, CO: Marzano Research.

Massachusetts Department of Elementary and Secondary Education. (2011, March). *Massachusetts curriculum framework for English language arts and literacy, grades pre-kindergarten to 12: Incorporating the Common Core State Standards for English language arts and literacy in history/social studies, science, and technical subjects.* Malden, MA: Author.

Mattos, M., & Buffum, A. (Eds.). (2015). *It's about time: Planning interventions and extensions in secondary school.* Bloomington, IN: Solution Tree Press.

McLaughlin, M. W., & Talbert, J. E. (2006). *Building school-based teacher learning communities: Professional strategies to improve student achievement.* New York: Teachers College Press.

McNulty, R. J., & Gloeckler, L. C. (2011, February). *Fewer, clearer, higher Common Core State Standards: Implications for students receiving special education services* [White paper]. Rexford, NY: International Center for Leadership in Education. Accessed at http://teacher.scholastic.com/products/scholastic-achievement-partners/downloads/SpecialEd_CCSS.pdf on December 10, 2015.

Mellard, D., & National Research Center on Learning Disabilities. (2006, March 2). *Integrating IDEA provisions with school reform: EIS and RTI.* Presented at the IDEA Partnership Meeting, Arlington, VA.

National Center for Education Statistics. (n.d.). *NAEP [National Assessment of Educational Progress] data explorer.* Accessed at https://nces.ed.gov/nationsreportcard/lttdata on December 10, 2015.

National Council for the Social Studies. (2010). *National curriculum standards for social studies: A framework for teaching, learning, and assessment.* Silver Spring, MD: Author.

National Governors Association Center for Best Practices & Council of Chief State School Officers. (n.d.a). *About the standards.* Accessed at www.corestandards.org/about-the-standards on December 4, 2015.

National Governors Association Center for Best Practices & Council of Chief State School Officers. (n.d.b). *Application to students with disabilities.* Washington, DC: Authors. Accessed at www.corestandards.org/wp-content/uploads/Application-to-Students-with-Disabilities-again-for-merge1.pdf on September 21, 2015.

National Governors Association Center for Best Practices & Council of Chief State School Officers. (2010a). *Common Core State Standards for English language arts and literacy in history/social studies, science, and technical subjects.* Washington, DC: Authors. Accessed at www.corestandards.org/wp-content/uploads/ELA_Standards.pdf on August 18, 2015.

National Governors Association Center for Best Practices & Council of Chief State School Officers. (2010b). *Common Core State Standards for mathematics.* Washington, DC: Authors. Accessed at www.corestandards.org/wp-content/uploads/Math_Standards.pdf on August 18, 2015.

National Research Council. (2002). *Executive summary: Disproportionate representation of minority students in special education.* Washington, DC: Author.

Perkins-Gough, D. (2013). The significance of grit: A conversation with Angela Lee Duckworth. *Educational Leadership, 71*(1), 14–20.

Pfeffer, J., & Sutton, R. I. (2000). *The knowing-doing gap: How smart companies turn knowledge into action.* Boston: Harvard Business School Press.

Popham, W. J. (2007). All about accountability: The lowdown on learning progressions. *Educational Leadership, 64*(7), 83–84.

Popham, W. J. (2008). *Transformative assessment.* Alexandria, VA: Association for Supervision and Curriculum Development.

President's Commission on Excellence in Special Education. (2002, July). *A new era: Revitalizing special education for children and their families.* Washington, DC: U.S. Department of Education.

Reeves, D. (2002). *The leader's guide to standards: A blueprint for educational equity and excellence.* San Francisco: Jossey-Bass.

Reeves, D. (Ed.). (2007). *Ahead of the curve: The power of assessment to transform teaching and learning.* Bloomington, IN: Solution Tree Press.

Samuels, C. A. (2011). Special educators look to tie IEPs to Common Core: Standards adoptions buoy long-running efforts to tie IEPs to academic benchmarks. *Education Week, 30*(15), 8–9.

Saphier, J. (2005). *John Adams' promise: How to have good schools for all our children, not just for some.* Acton, MA: Research for Better Teaching.

Schmoker, M., & Marzano, R. J. (1999). Realizing the promise of standards-based education. *Educational Leadership, 56*(6), 17–21.

Shanahan, T. (2011, August 21). *Rejecting instructional level theory.* Accessed at www.shanahanonliteracy.com/2011/08/rejecting-instructional-level-theory.html on September 23, 2015.

Shanahan, T. (2014a, April 29). *Re-thinking reading interventions.* Accessed at www .shanahanonliteracy.com/2014/04/re-thinking-reading-interventions.html on September 23, 2015.

Shanahan, T. (2014b, September 30). *Snappy responses on challenging text debate.* Accessed at www.shanahanonliteracy.com/2014/09/snappy-responses-on -challenging-text.html on August 18, 2015.

Stark, P., Noel, A. M., & McFarland, J. (2015, June). *Trends in high school dropout and completion rates in the United States: 1972–2012.* Washington, DC: National Center for Education Statistics. Accessed at http://nces.ed.gov/pubs2015 /2015015.pdf on August 18, 2015.

Strauss, V. (2014, September 22). Common Core calls for kids to read books that 'frustrate' them. Is that a good idea? *Washington Post.* Accessed at www .washingtonpost.com/blogs/answer-sheet/wp/2014/09/22/common-core-calls-for -kids-to-read-books-that-frustrate-them-is-that-a-good-idea on August 18, 2015.

Thurlow, M. L. (2011, August). *Common Core State Standards: Implications for students with disabilities* [PowerPoint slides]. Accessed at http://ncscpartners.org/Media /Default/PDFs/Resources/Thurlow-CCSS-SWD-8-2011.pdf on August 18, 2015.

Thurlow, M. L., Quenemoen, R. F., & Lazarus, S. S. (2012). Leadership for student performance in an era of accountability. In J. B. Crockett, B. S. Billingsley, & M. L. Boscardin (Eds.), *Handbook of leadership and administration for special education* (pp. 3–16). New York: Routledge.

University of Kansas Center for Research on Learning. (2009). *Learning strategies.* Accessed at www.kucrl.org/sim/strategies.shtml on November 29, 2015.

U.S. Department of Education. (n.d.). *ED data express: Data about elementary and secondary schools in the U.S.* Accessed at http://eddataexpress.ed.gov/data-elements .cfm/tool/trend on December 10, 2015.

U.S. Department of Education. (2014, December). *36th annual report to Congress on the implementation of the* Individuals With Disabilities Education Act, *2014.* Washington, DC: U.S. Department of Education, Office of Special Education and Rehabilitative Services, Office of Special Education Programs. Accessed at www2 .ed.gov/about/reports/annual/osep/2014/parts-b-c/36th-idea-arc.pdf on December 10, 2015.

Webb, N. L. (2002, March 28). *Depth-of-knowledge levels for four content areas* [Unpublished paper]. Accessed at www.hed.state.nm.us/uploads/files/ABE /Policies/depth_of_knowledge_guide_for_all_subject_areas.pdf on December 10, 2015.

Wood, D., Bruner, J. S., & Ross, G. (1976). The role of tutoring in problem solving. *Journal of Child Psychology and Psychiatry, 17*(2), 89–100.

Yudin, M. (2014, June 25). *Higher expectations to better outcomes for children with disabilities.* Accessed at http://blog.ed.gov/2014/06/higher-expectations-to-better -outcomes-for-children-with-disabilities on December 1, 2015.

Index

A

achievement gaps, 8
Allen, R., 71, 72
Armstrong, T., 67
assessments
    aligning instruction and, 78
    continuum of, 76–77
    developing, 79–80
    pre-, 84–85
    views on, 75

B

Bailey, K., 43, 47
Baker, S., 59
Brown, J. E., 99–100
Buffum, A., 97
building-level teams, 18, 21–23
Bush, G. W., 9

C

Childress, S. M., 41
Clifton, D. O., 66–67
Collaborating for Success With the Common Core: A Toolkit for Professional Learning Communities at Work (Bailey, Jakicic, & Spiller), 43
collaboration
    at the elementary level, 17–24
    professional development and, 27–28
    at secondary levels, 24–27
Common Core State Standards (CCSS), 14, 43
    instructional shifts, defining, 63–66
Common Formative Assessment: A Toolkit for Professional Learning Communities at Work (Bailey & Jakicic), 43
content-alike teams, 25, 26–27
Council of Chief State School Officers (CCSSO), 14
cross-curricular teams, 25–26
"Cultural, Linguistic, and Ecological Framework for Response to Intervention With English Language Learners, A" (Brown & Doolittle), 99
curriculum
    See also guaranteed and viable curriculum
    chaos and action steps, 42–62
    designing a specialized, 80–81
    differences in establishing, 41–42
    resources, 43

D

destructive struggle, 71–72
Diamond, K. E., 10
discrepancy model, 10, 12

Doolittle, J., 99–100

Douglass, F., 71

Doyle, D. P., 41

dropout rates, 8

Duckworth, A., 55–56

DuFour, R., 1, 30, 97

E

Eaker, R., 1

elementary level, collaboration and, 17–24

F

Fuchs, L. S., 59

G

Gersten, R., 59

goals

    collecting data aligned to, 95

    planning, 85–92

Goethe, J. W., 63

grade-level teams, 18, 19–21

guaranteed and viable curriculum

    See also curriculum

    action steps for establishing, 42–62

    defined, 29

    indicators of, 30–33

    materials and resources, determining, 69–70

    prioritizing standards, 45–45, 110–111

    selecting units/topics, 44–45

    unpacking priority standards, 46–62, 112

H

Harter, J. K., 66–67

I

independent functioning, 34–36

individualized education program (IEP)

    goals, 11, 84

    planning, 85–92

    tool for discussion guide, 115–116

    tool to determine, 113–114

Individuals With Disabilities Education Act (IDEA), 8, 10, 12, 98

instruction for students with special needs

    aligning assessment and, 78

    plans, examples of, 85, 86–87

    tailoring, 66–73

instructional shifts, defining, 63–66

It's About Time: Planning Interventions and Extensions in Elementary School (Buffum and Mattos), 97

J

Jackson, R. R., 71, 72

Jakicic, C., 43, 47

job-alike, cross-school teams

    at the elementary level, 18, 23–24

    at the secondary level, 25, 27

Justice, L. M., 10

K

Kaldenberg, E. R., 59

Keenon, J., 59

Kennedy, M., 20–21

Kildeer Countryside Community
Consolidated School District
96, 12, 13, 20, 35, 59

L

Lambert, C., 71

Lazarus, S. S., 15

leadership teams. *See* building-level
teams

learning levels, ensuring high, 36–37

learning progression, determining,
55–57, 69

learning targets
defined, 47
identifying, 49–51

Little, J. W., 83

low-incidence conditions, 35

M

Many, T. W., 1

Marzano, R. J., 12, 29, 30–31, 42, 54

Mattos, M., 97

McLaughlin, M. W., 17

N

National Center for Learning
Disabilities, 9

National Governors Association Center
for Best Practices, 14

*Neurodiversity in the Classroom:
Strength-Based Strategies to Help
Students With Special Needs
Succeed in School and Life*
(Anderson), 67

*New Area: Revitalizing Special Education
for Children and Their Families,
A*, 9

P

PLCs (professional learning
communities)
defined, 1
ideas of, 1
questions of, 2
response to intervention and, 100,
103–106

Popham, W. J., 55, 57, 75

President's Commission on Excellence
in Special Education, 7, 9–14

prioritizing standards, 45–46, 110–111

priority standards
identifying, 47–48
unpacking, 46–62, 69, 112

problem-solving discussion tool, 91

problem-solving teams. *See* building-
level teams

productive struggle, 71–72

professional development, collaboration
and, 27–28

professional development for special
education teachers, need for, 11

professional learning communities. *See*
PLCs

progress monitoring
fine-tuning, 92–95
planning goals and, 85–92

Q

Quenemoen, R. F., 15

R

Reeves, D., 110

response to intervention (RTI)

improving instruction to close gaps, 100–102

legislation, 12, 98–100

professional learning communities and, 100, 103–106

rigor, determining levels of, 51–53

Ruff, L., 26

S

Saphier, J., 14, 30

scaffolds and supports, determining, 57–62, 70–71

Schmoker, M., 42

schoolwide cultural shifts, 33–34

secondary levels, collaboration and, 24–27

Shanahan, T., 70

Siegler, R. S., 10

Simple as 1, 2, 3: The Prioritizing Process, 45–46, 110–111

Snyder, P. A., 10

special education

closing the gap, commitment to, 16

history of, 7–15

separate from general education system, 11

Spiller, J., 43

standards

prioritizing, 45–46, 110–111

unpacking priority, 46–62, 69, 112

students with special needs

beliefs about learning and responsibilities for, 14–15

independent functioning, 34–36

tailoring instruction for, 66–73

who are, 8–9

T

Talbert, J. E., 17

text complexity, 70–71

Therrien, W. J., 59

Thomas, D. A., 41

Thurlow, M. L., 15

U

U.S. Department of Education, Office of Special Education, 8, 9

University of Kansas, Center for Research on Learning, 59

unpacking priority standards, 46–62, 69, 112

V

verbs (skills) and knowledge (concepts), identifying, 48–49

vocabulary, identifying key, 53–55

W

Watt, S. J., 59

Webb's Depth of Knowledge (DOK), 51–53

Williams, J. P., 59

Y

Yudin, M., 66

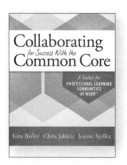

Collaborating for Success With the Common Core
Kim Bailey, Chris Jakicic, and Jeanne Spiller
Leverage teamwork to integrate the CCSS into your curriculum, and build on a foundational knowledge of PLCs. You'll gain a comprehensive understanding of the shifts required to implement the standards in core content areas and find tips and strategies for strong collaborative practices.
BKF556

Common Formative Assessment
Kim Bailey and Chris Jakicic
The catalyst for real student improvement begins with a decision to implement common formative assessments. In this conversational guide, the authors offer tools, templates, and protocols to incorporate common formative assessments into the practices of a PLC to monitor and enhance student learning.
BKF538

Learning by Doing, 3rd Edition
Richard DuFour, Rebecca DuFour, Robert Eaker, and Thomas Many
Discover how to transform your school or district into a high-performing PLC. The third edition of this comprehensive action guide offers new strategies for addressing critical PLC topics, including hiring and retaining new staff, creating team-developed common formative assessments, and more.
BKF746

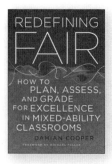

Redefining Fair
Damian Cooper
Learn how to define proficiency accurately and differentiate to help all students achieve it. Using stories, strategies, case histories, and sample documents, the author explains how to implement equitable instruction, assessment, grading, and reporting practices for diverse 21st century learners.
BKF412

Solution Tree | Press
a division of

Solution Tree

Visit solution-tree.com or call 800.733.6786 to order.

"Tremendous, tremendous, tremendous!

The speaker made me do some very deep internal reflection about the **PLC process** and the personal responsibility I have in making the school improvement process work **for ALL kids.**"

PD Services

Our experts draw from decades of research and their own experiences to bring you practical strategies for building and sustaining a high-performing PLC. You can choose from a range of customizable services, from a one-day overview to a multiyear process.

Book your PLC PD today!
888.763.9045

Solution Tree